M000028870

Noise.
Hurry.
Crowds.

Noise.
Hurry.
Crowds.

On Creating Space for **God**
Amidst the Chaos of
Campus and Culture

Guy Chmieleski

Copyright 2015 by Guy Chmieleski

All rights reserved. No part of this publication may be reproduced, stored in a retrieval system, or transmitted, in any form or by any means—electronic, mechanical, photocopying, recording, or otherwise—without prior written permission, except for brief quotations in critical reviews or articles.

All Scripture quotations, unless otherwise indicated, are taken from HOLY BIBLE, NEW INTERNATIONAL VERSION®. Copyright © 1973, 1978, 1984 by International Bible Society. Used by permission of Zondervan. All rights reserved.

In contemporary society our Adversary majors in three things: noise, hurry, and crowds. If he can keep us engaged in "muchness" and "manyness," he will rest satisfied.
—Richard Foster, *Celebration of Discipline*

But just as he who called you is holy, so be holy in all you do; for it is written: "Be holy, because I am holy."
—1 Peter 1:15–16

Contents

Foreword

About a decade ago I submitted a proposal to a prominent publisher outlining a book that would focus on ministry with college students. Though favorable to the request, the publisher was uncertain whether there was a market sizeable enough to support the publishing of a book focused solely on what was regarded as a niche population. He suggested that I begin by creating a web presence to build up enough of a following to warrant such a publication. Guy Chmieleski, with his blogosphere, *Faith On Campus,* has created just such a venue. Bolstered by the e-publishing support of the wildly successful emergence of Seedbed as a gathering place for Wesleyan thought, Guy has found a medium for popularizing current thought and practice in theological circles and packaging it in such a way that it speaks into the college experience.

It is evident in his writing that Guy has tuned his heart to many of the contemporary spiritual masters—Richard Foster, Dallas Willard, Henri Nouwen, Robert Mulholland, and the like. Guy has a keen eye for knowing the maladies of college students that diminish their spiritual zeal and take away their saltiness.

In *Noise. Hurry. Crowds.*, Guy draws from the well of his own life experience to offer spiritual counsel to young adult believers. The result is a book that is readable, engaging, and offers one of the most critical needs for contemporary Christians today—a discerning mind to recognize the subtle ways that the seeds of the kingdom get choked out by the worries, cares, and enticements of this world. His call is the call that echoes throughout the pages of sacred script—"Choose life!" And do so by cultivating the desires of the heart through spiritual practices. Recognizing how toxic noise, hurry, and crowds can be to the soul of a college student, Guy advocates for disciplines of silence, Sabbath, solitude, and simplicity.

There are places in *Noise. Hurry. Crowds.* where Guy may jar you with a statement that seems unorthodox or even bordering on misappropriating a conventional truth—such as "the disciplines are not about God, but about us" or "the invitation to seek the kingdom of God is an invitation to do nothing." So you will need to read beyond the first appearance to hear what the author is trying to convey and to place such lines in the context of the whole book. What you will find immediately helpful are the fresh ways Guy names particular seductions of the soul like "visual noise," "assessing your own noise imprint," and becoming mindful of inner chatter. I think you will also be inspired by the practical ways Guy calls you to such practicalities as "calendar sacrifice" and "looking for little solitudes."

After reading *Noise. Hurry. Crowds.*, I reflected on my college days living in the dorm at a large state university in the South. During my freshman and sophomore years I lived in a dorm surrounded by a lively and diverse group of students. The cast of characters included: Bob—a Yugoslavian body builder who often had two cans of tuna fish for lunch; Ralph—a part Cherokee Indian who referred to everyone else as "Chief"; Sal—a Hispanic who flexed his calves every step until they looked like overgrown inverted jalepeños; Drew—a disaffiliated Catholic who knocked on my door once sleep walking; and others who were fully embroiled in the escapades of college life. And then there was Lee.

Lee was a medical student who was awed by studying anatomy and biology, fascinated with what he found of God's design in something like the structure of a cell. Systematically, Lee found a chance to share the gospel with almost every person on the floor, sometimes earning only verbal abuse for his efforts. I was impressed with the steadiness of Lee's life, the rigor of his study, and the resiliency he exhibited to endure rejection for the sake of Christ. I watched Lee, wondering what deep wells were sustaining his spirit and vivifying his life. I don't think I would have had Guy Chmieleski's four practices at that time to measure Lee's life, but in hindsight, I think they formed much of his anchor.

Lee lived without a roommate, thus creating some modicum of *silence* and *solitude* amidst the noise of the dorm. His room served as both study and sanctuary; he was as disciplined in his devotional life as he was with his studies. Unlike most dorm rooms, I don't recall seeing a giant stereo in Lee's room blaring music, nor do I recall posters on the wall or other memorabilia reflecting the visual noise of culture. Lee's room was noteworthy for its *simplicity,* evidence that there was not much opportunity for clutter or diversion. I am not sure that I ever asked Lee about his practice of Sabbath, but I suspect he was pretty regular in finding respite time to connect with those of kindred heart and mind.

Lee was for me a city set on a hill—a beacon of light in a world otherwise saturated with loud, frenetic energy that usually diffused into nothingness and where lives collided like billiard balls but rarely meaningfully related. I believe in the importance of what Guy writes because I have seen the fruit of it in a fellow compatriot. If you will learn the lessons of this book, you too will find that life can be ordered on two planes and that beneath the noise, hurry, and crowds there is a Friend who sticks closer than a brother.

Chris A. Kiesling, PhD
Professor of Human Development
and Christian Discipleship
Asbury Theological Seminary

Acknowledgments

What a gift it is to think and write and share about things that matter, about things that shape life and meaning and purpose. Projects like these are never (at least not for me) a work in isolation. There are so many people who have helped in the process—or helped in my own development and formation along the way. So it's only appropriate to start with a few brief words of thanks.

To Seedbed, thanks for believing in this project, and continuing to believe in me. I love sowing seeds of grace and truth and love with you all. May God continue to bless our relationship and produce much fruit from all your good work.

To those who have helped model a different way—a better way—of life in this world, I owe you a tremendous debt of gratitude. While there are many who have done this in their own unique and distinct ways, Ben, you deserve a special word of thanks for your consistent willingness to create space for me to deal with my own noise, hurry, and crowds. I cherish your care, counsel, and finely tuned listening ear.

To my wife, Heather, thanks for being a steadfast reminder of what's most important in life and challenging me to live accordingly. And to my kids—Derek, Autumn,

Kaiya, Noll, and Lailie Grace—thanks for consistently calling me back from the things I allow to distract me, especially when my attentions should be on you. You make me a better dad and I love being yours!

Finally, I give thanks to Jesus, who daily invites me (and invites us all) to live life with peace, presence, poise, grace, and love in a world that is in need of these things in abundance. Lord, have your way with us all.

Introduction

May 14, 2014. Yesterday I announced that I was starting work on this book. I made my announcement the way most people do such things, or attempt to share anything with the world at large anymore; I posted an image of my title page to some of my favorite social media sites. (Yes, I understand the irony given the focus of this book.)

One shares in this way, I suppose, for a variety of reasons.

Yes, to declare to the world that we are going to attempt something—something big and important—something beyond ourselves. But also, I believe, we do it to gain the collective support and encouragement of those who might take notice of this declaration because we know that we're desperately going to need it.

Of course, I was pleased to receive a number of uplifting comments and words of affirmation throughout the day (social media sharing success!), but it was the interaction I had via Twitter with a former student of mine that led me to believe I was actually on to something.

Our Twitter conversation went something like this:

ME: Starting a new writing project today. #timetowrite #workingtitle

@formerstudent: Nice! Wish you would have written that a few years ago! One of the biggest struggles I had in college!

@ME: Hey @formerstudent! Good to hear from you! The question I have is: What would have gotten you to slow down long enough to read it?

@formerstudent: Maybe someone recognizing my frenzied life, using the book like a stop sign, and smacking me over the head. Maybe then . . .

@ME: So you're telling me there's a chance (of getting the attention of today's students)??? ☺

@formerstudent: Only if you go around campus smacking kids in the face with the book! ☺

What struck me most about our Twitter chat was the fact that I had known this student to be among the cream of the crop while he was on campus. He was a stellar student and leader. He was an engaged student who took his academics more serious than most. And although he was clearly busy, he appeared to have a better handle on the distractions of life than most of his peers.

If he confessed to me that this was a major struggle for him, then I've got to believe it was all the more so for many of his peers, who seemed to be much less aware of the fact that they were indeed living distracted lives.

Can you relate? Does this sound like the kind of existence you are attempting to lead? Does it feel like living? Or is it more like you're just holding on?

In more recent years, I've talked with a growing number of students who struggle with regret over the priorities they've chosen—that have been shaping their life in recent months, or in some cases, throughout their entire college career.

This Distracted Life

Hey. Hey! Thanks for picking up this book and getting this far into it.

Oh, I know you're just a couple of pages into the introduction. *No*, I'm not trying to offend you. I've just come to realize that getting the attention of a college student in the twenty-first century is a lot harder than it once was. And I also know that picking up a book that's not required reading during college doesn't happen as much as it once did either.

No, this isn't a lament for the days that once were. Although, there seems to come a time for every generation when they look back toward what felt like a more simple kind of existence and recognize how much more complex life has become, and they wonder, *What if?*

But I digress.

What's clear to me is that life today is *louder, faster,* and *more congested* than it ever has been in my lifetime—and yours too. There is so much that vies for our attention. There's so much that we can give our focus, our time, our money, and make our priority. With an overabundance of options and opportunities, you might think that life has gotten better or easier, but I would argue that's not so. While some advances and evolutions may make more possible, or life more convenient, I believe that we are increasingly living a distracted kind of existence.

What we don't seem to realize amidst the array of distractions that we confront (or even create for ourselves) is that what we are ultimately being distracted from is not the problems, pressures, or pain of our lives (although that may happen temporarily), but God and the kind of *full life* that he desires for us.

You see, there's a power—a force—behind the distractions we encounter in this life. Richard Foster referred to this force as "our Adversary" in the quote on the opening pages of this book. The Bible refers to this same master of distraction as Satan, or the Devil. Take a moment to flip back and reread that quote. Our Adversary is using the cultural distractions of noise, hurry, crowds, and the pursuit of "muchness" and "manyness" to keep our focus and attention fixated on the things of this world. He is against us and wants us to give up on the With-God life.

The Adversary is our enemy. He does not want us walking closely with God. And he's smart enough to know that a full-on frontal attack would likely be too obvious, and might cause us to cry out for God's grace and assistance in ways he cannot combat—so he has to be subtle, cunning, and deceptive. He knows that if he can distract us with things that seem good, or okay, or normal by our societal standards, then he believes that we're as good as defeated—and what's worse is that most of us don't even know it.

Growing Up in a Culture of Distraction

The world has become an increasingly noisy, fast-paced, and crowded place to exist. You may not be able to see this in the same ways that I do, or your parents or professors can, because you've grown up with many of the advances in technology and cultural priorities that make life today feel so frenetic. But for those of us older than forty, we can remember a time before cell phones, social media, YouTube, and the Internet. We can remember a time when leisure and play seemed to be more of a priority. We can remember a time when social interaction only happened between people—face-to-face—and your friends were people you spent quality time with on a regular basis.

Does this sound anything like the world you've grown up in? Probably not. You've grown up in a digital world—full of screens, conveniences, and opportunities that are still relatively new to the world. And there is a lot that we still don't know with regard to how all of these "advances" are changing us as they change our world. But one thing we can say for sure is that all of the advances and new technologies are creating a new way of life—a life filled with new complexities and distractions that make keeping our eyes on God a real challenge.

It reminds me of a story from the Bible found in the book of Daniel. I see great similarities between our increasingly noisy, hurried, and crowded world and the Israelite exiles who were once carried off into the foreign land of Babylon to live among the gods and cultural priorities of a people who did not know the One True God. And you—you and your generation—you are like the youth who were born and raised in this foreign land. You hear a lot of stories about life "back in the day," but likely do not have firsthand experience of what life was like without all of today's conveniences and cultural distractions. Life has changed a great deal in the last thirty years, and your parents, pastors, and professors were raised in a time that was drastically different. It had its own set of challenges to be sure, but many of the complexities that you know as normal were not a part of our youth. We're trying to adapt to life in the twenty-first century, hopefully in ways that are healthy and make good sense, but this is the only life you've known.

The adoption of noise, hurry, and crowds as a normal way of life wasn't a quick shift, but more of a slow fade. At first it took the form of minor accommodation for those who chose a different way of life. It was a way of life that seemed to be designated to a smaller part of the population that had priorities that were ambitious, opportunistic, and cutting-edge. And somewhere along the way, what was once accommodation increasingly became the new normal. Not only did it become the new normal, but this noisy, hurried, crowded—distracted—way of life managed to become the more *preferred* and even celebrated way of life.

We now have come to believe that if you're not plugged-in, racing from one thing to another, and in constant contact with your friends (or followers), then something must be wrong with *you*.

In North America, with all of our advances in technology (coupled with the ways in which we deify things like power, fame, wealth, status, and influence) we've created a noisy, hurried, and crowded way of life that drowns out the still, small voice of God. Our pursuits, pleasures, and people have become the very things that the Enemy uses to keep our gaze focused on the things of this earth and averted from the With-God life.

And you've spent eighteen plus years growing up in this kind of culture before heading off to college. You've left behind some of those "original exiles," maybe your parents or pastors who had firsthand experienced with a more simple way of life, and quite possibly a more intentional way of living the With-God life, who were doing their best to educate you about how you, too, could live more intentionally in an increasingly complex world. A life that looks much less like the culture around us, which does not seem to have much of an awareness of God, and looks much more holy and set apart.

Distractions Magnified on Campus

The cultural distractions of noise, hurry, crowds, and the pursuit of muchness and manyness only seem to be amplified once you arrive on campus.

Again, I point us back to the reality of an Adversary who is cunning and deceptive, and who knows that if he can get you to avert your gaze even slightly, to change your priorities or compromise on your convictions early on in your college experience, that you will head down a path that will lead you away from God—and you'll be unlikely to ever look back.

The college years are some of the most formative of your life. Did you know that? It's true. In fact, many psychologists and sociologists believe that behind the toddler years—years when you are learning to walk and talk—the college years are the years that you are most profoundly shaped and formed in your life. And if you think about it, it makes sense. You've just moved away from the family that you've spent the majority of your life with. You've moved away from other long-standing influences in your life—pastors, educators, neighbors, employers, coaches, leaders, and friends. You're in a season of substantial transition.

You've now taken up residence in a new enviroment—designed to engage your mind and challenge many of your preconceived notions about, well, most of life. You're surrounded by new voices—educators who are among the top in their field and who may or may not have a care in the world about your faith development as a part of the college experience. And you're also living with a random assortment of fellow peers—who you now spend the majority of your time with at home, in class, and socializing. These new peers come from all over the world and will likely vary in what they believe and how they live in both small and large ways.

Times of transition tend to be a fertile ground for considering and reconsidering much of life. *The Enemy knows this.* But God is the one who created life to be like this. Transitions aren't a time to consider giving up or walking away from our faith; they are a time for leaning into God and experiencing him in the midst of change and uncertainty.

But God will not force himself on you. He never has and he never will.

That's not who God is. It's not how he works.

A God Who Wants Us to Want Him— More Than Anything Else

The Old Testament is a collection of stories of how God loved and interacted with the Israelites. All people were God's people, because he was (and is) the Creator of all. But the Israelites were special. They were God's chosen people. God wanted the Israelites to be a living example to the rest of the world of the With-God life. He wanted them to model sacrifice, obedience, and loving-kindness, and to be an example of the kind of blessings that came with being in relationship with the One True God.

But the Old Testament tells the sordid tale of a people—God's holy and chosen people—struggling to fully commit to him. We see God give the Israelites second, third, fourth chances and more. But his chosen people struggle to be faithful. They struggle to keep their focus on him. They are often distracted by the numerous noises of their day—and therefore easily led astray. Instead of being the shining example that God desired, the Israelites more often reflected the cultural priorities and lifestyles of the cultures around them. Much like many of us Christians do today.

God did not give up on his creation even though he had plenty of reason to. We see God's unwavering commitment to his children throughout the biblical narrative, but exemplified most clearly in the coming of Jesus. Instead of backing out, staying away, or starting over, we see God double-down on his efforts to win the hearts of his people. He chose to come to earth in the person of Jesus—to repair the damaged relationship between God and his creation, and to model for us a way of living the With-God life. And even upon Jesus' death his efforts were not finished. Instead, we read that he went to sit at the right hand of God to serve as an Advocate on our behalf. We also read that he sent the Holy Spirit to serve as a comforter and guide. And that same Spirit is still present among us, and within us, as God's created.

But God still wants us to want him. God wants us to choose him—every day. God wants us to want him more than we want anything else and then to reflect that in how we order our lives.

Again, God won't force himself on us. He never has and he never will. But this is where a lot of us get stuck.

The Gift of Experiencing God through Spiritual Disciplines

If you're anything like me, when you've previously been a part of classes or conversations talking about a relationship with God—and how you *do* that—the vast majority of what you've heard is some rendition of, "just read your Bible and pray." Just read your Bible and pray. It sounds easy enough, and yet, if you've ever spent much time really trying to give this your very best effort, you know that eventually you can come to a place where you feel like you get stuck. Or you struggle to find the text as engaging as you once did. Or you wonder if your prayers are making it past the ceiling of your room. You are making an earnest effort to pursue God through the measures that have been prescribed to you, but even your very best efforts feel like they're coming up short.

And once these struggles begin they can be difficult to overcome.

I don't believe God wants us to fixate on these two pathways for knowing and experiencing him. He's so much bigger and greater than we can possibly imagine, so to believe that we can follow such rote rituals and expect that we will be able to consistently experience—and ultimately know—the Divine, is unreasonable.

And yet, most churches and families that I've encountered don't speak of much beyond, "just read your Bible and pray."

But what if I told you there were actually some practices that have been around for centuries upon centuries that speak to a wide variety of ways by which we might pursue, encounter, and experience God? Would you believe me? I promise it's true! Most people who know about these ways refer to them as spiritual disciplines. Author Richard Foster referred to them as, "God's means of grace."[1] I love that. On the means of grace, American philosopher Dallas Willard stated:

> They are disciplines designed to help us be active and effective in the spiritual realm of our own heart, now spiritually alive by grace, in relation to God and his kingdom. They are designed to help us withdraw from total dependence on the merely human or natural . . . and to depend also on the ultimate reality, which is God and his kingdom.[2]

This sounds great, and yet the author of the book of Hebrews gives us this cautionary word as we consider moving forward, "No discipline seems pleasant at the time, but painful. Later on, however, it produces a harvest of righteousness and peace for those who have been trained by it" (Heb. 12:11).

Steps Toward Grace

Here's where things can get a little tricky. We want the love, intimacy, and connection that come with having a growing and dynamic relationship with Jesus. But all we've ever been told (if even taught) is to read our Bible and pray. So upon learning about spiritual disciplines we might be inclined to throw down this book and pick up something that can give us the lowdown on spiritual disciplines. We've identified the root of our spiritual struggles, now let's master the solution!

But before you do, give me to the end of this introduction.

We'll get to the disciplines, but first we need to explore some more manageable pieces to this new puzzle. In some respects, it's similar to learning about running and maybe training for a 5k race before you attempt to train for that first half- or full-marathon. If you've never been a runner you could do a lot of physical (not to mention mental) damage to yourself if you go out and attempt a ten or twelve mile run on your first day as a new runner. You could wreck yourself before you ever really begin.

Don't get me wrong. The spiritual disciplines are not only for the spiritually elite. They're not only for the spiritual giants, the religiously learned, or the monastically motivated. Spiritual disciplines are for people like you and people like me. Foster said it this way:

> God intends the Disciplines of the spiritual life to be for ordinary human beings: people who have jobs, who care for children, who wash dishes and mow lawns. In fact, the Disciplines are best exercised in the midst of our relationships with our husband or wife, our brothers and sisters, our friends and neighbors.[3]

So the spiritual disciplines are for everyone. But they do require new levels of awareness, understanding, commitment, and dedication. Once we begin to journey with God down new pathways provided by our engagement of some new spiritual exercises, we will no longer be content to return to the rote routines of simply reading our Bibles and praying. And your first thought might be, *Well, who would ever want to do that?* But the truth of the matter is that we like our routines and rhythms. We like things that are easy and come naturally to us. And you should also know that our practice of the different spiritual disciplines does not guarantee us anything.

In much the same way that simply reading our Bible and praying once created a pathway for genuine encounters and intimacy with God, that pathway eventually felt like it ceased to provide a tangible connection. The truth is that there's no magic formula to relating to God. There's no promise that what seems to draw us near to the heart of God on one day will recreate the same (or even similar) kind of experience ever again. If they did, we would be in a position where we could manipulate God to do as we wished (or at least provide us with a consistent feeling of spiritual connectedness).

Instead, the disciplines are designed to put us in a position, or a posture, to better experience God. They have everything to do with preparing our head and our heart to encounter the Holy—should the Holy choose to encounter us.

Doing the Work That Only We Can Do And Leaving the Rest to God

The spiritual disciplines are the work that we do. Our work is important—even significant. But it does have limitations.

The apostle Paul captured this reality for us brilliantly in the midst of a rebuke he once gave the Christians in Corinth who were fighting about to whom they owed their allegiance—Paul or Barnabas. Paul knew the foolishness of their dispute and painted this vivid picture to make his point clear:

> Brothers and sisters, I could not address you as people who live by the Spirit but as people who are still worldly— mere infants in Christ. I gave you milk, not solid food, for you were not yet ready for it. Indeed, you are still not ready. You are still worldly. For since there is jealousy and quarreling among you, are you not worldly? Are you not acting like mere humans? For when one says, "I follow Paul," and another, "I follow Apollos," are you not mere human beings?

> What, after all, is Apollos? And what is Paul? Only servants, through whom you came to believe—as the Lord has assigned to each his task. I planted the seed, Apollos watered it, but God has been making it grow. So neither the one who plants nor the one who waters is anything, but only God, who makes things grow. The one who plants and the one who waters have one purpose, and they will each be rewarded according to their own labor. For we are co-workers in God's service; you are God's field, God's building. (1 Cor. 3:1–9)

Paul knew full well that neither he, nor Barnabas, were much of anything without the power of God working through them. He didn't deny that they each played a role. But he clearly knew that their human roles had limitations—and it was a role given to each of them by God. Paul and Barnabas both played a role in the process—the process of the new Christians in Corinth growing in Christ—but it was God who made things grow.

The same is true of you and me when we engage in the practice of spiritual disciplines. We play a role in our own spiritual formation. But that role does have limitations. And while we might be tempted to believe that we can just sit back and let God do all of the work, we would be mistaken. Willard wrote, "Reliance upon what the Spirit does to us or in us, as indispensable as it truly is, will not by itself transform character in its depths. The action of the Spirit must be accompanied by our response."[4] We do our work and God does his work.

We play a role in our own spiritual growth and development. We actively participate in our personal relationship with Jesus—for what is a relationship, after all, if not something we are meant to actively participate in?

The Goal: A With-God Life

If you're still reading this book, then I think you want what I want. You want what the vast majority of Christians who profess a faith in Christ want. A close, personal, intimate relationship with the One True God. To know and know that we are truly known by the King of kings and Lord of lords. It's about so much more than where we will spend our eternity—although that's significant as well. It's about living this present life with God.

It's the With-God life we've been talking about throughout this introduction—and will continue to talk about throughout the rest of this book.

There are three distinct phases that I think we must engage as we pursue the With-God life. The first has to do with beginning to better control and take care of the world in which we live. No, I'm not talking creation care—although that is important—it's just not the focus of this book.

What I'm talking about is the noise, hurry, and crowds that constantly overwhelm our lives. It's our obsession with muchness and manyness. To use Paul's metaphor of the farmer or gardener, our first work must be to tend to the soil of our own lives. We must start by tilling the earth of our soul and dealing with the weeds, pests, and other elements that would make growth impossible if left alone.

If we want the With-God life we must do the hard work of clearing out a lot of the junk that takes up unnecessary space in our minds, hearts, schedules, and lives. We must bring under control, with God's help, the noise, hurry, and crowds that so readily distract us. We must learn to deal with our unhealthy fixations on muchness and manyness.

This book is about learning how to better create and cultivate the kind of life that God can speak into—such that you might actually be able to hear him—because you're learning to deal with the distractions that have long served to crowd out his still, small voice.

As we begin to deal with these major distractions, I'll introduce you to four new spiritual disciplines that I believe God can use to transform your life—from the inside out. These four disciplines are meant to directly counter the issues of noise, hurry, crowds, and the pursuit of muchness and manyness. Not only that, but God can also use them to breathe new life into old (but incredibly important) practices, like Bible study and prayer. And although there are other spiritual disciplines we could add to this text, we will focus on the practices of silence, Sabbath, solitude, and simplicity.

Finally, I'll take some time to give you some easy entry points into these new practices—because there will be a learning curve, and you don't need to get overwhelmed as you embark on this new season of pursuing God and the With-God life.

Are you ready for this? Because everything changes once you turn this page.

Noise.
Hurry.
Crowds.

CHAPTER ONE

Noise

Okay. So you turned the page. That tells me one of two things: you're either *really* curious about how I would follow up such a dramatic conclusion to the introduction, *or* you've decided that you've had enough of living the quasi-Christian life and are ready to pursue definitive change. I'm hoping it's the latter.

It's not that your faith commitments have been half-hearted up to this point in your life. It's more likely that you've never been properly educated on, or equipped with, the resources that might help you achieve some of the desires you have for your relationship with God. The intimacy and depth you crave with Jesus is indeed possible, but it requires understanding what might be hindering you before even identifying what will move you toward what you desire—the very heart of God.

So let's start with one of the greatest cultural distractions of our day: noise.

Pump Up the Volume

Noise can be defined in a number of ways. It's more than the audible sound that our ears are attracted to—and the volume by which those sounds are projected—but that's definitely a part of our noisy world.

I believe noise can also be *visual*. The billboards, posters, street signs, marquees, and other visual attractions that are designed to grab our attention also serve to create a kind of noise in our lives. Then, of course, there is the wide array of screens that vie for our constant gaze: phones, tablets, computer screens, TVs, and more often than not, multiple screens at the same time. All begging for our attention.

Jun Young and David Kinnaman, authors of *The Hyperlinked Life*, have found that "Seventy-one percent of people feel overwhelmed by the amount of information they need to stay up to date."[1]

I also believe noise can be *mental*. I think it can come in the form of a cluttered mind—a mind that seems to run nonstop because of the overwhelming amount of information it is attempting to take in. It can also entail a vivid fantasy life that we escape to in order to pursue a form of artificial intimacy and/or hide from our present realities; or the frenetic playing and replaying of past or potential scenarios in our head—whether best case, worst case, or completely random.

Of course, this mental noise has a way of translating and transcending from our heads down into our hearts and causing us to live with an all too noisy *emotional* life as well. Feeling high strung, or tightly wound, can be both exhausting and nerve-racking. Too many of us live with high levels of anxiety and worry, believing that it's just a normal part of life. But it doesn't have to be. When the volume on our emotions is cranked up it can be near impossible to give any kind of focus or attention to anything else.

The Noise of the World

Our households and offices are filled with the whir-ring, buzzing, murmuring, chattering, and whining of the multiple contraptions that are supposed to make life easier. Their noise comforts us in some curious way. In fact, we find complete silence shocking because it leaves the impression that nothing is happening. In a go-go world such as ours, what could be worse than that![2]

These words were penned and published by Dallas Willard in 1988. He likely would have known of the Internet, but this would have been just before it was introduced to the wider world and well before computers were a common household (and later dorm room) item, and therefore before the inventions of things like social media and smart phones. That is a world you likely do not know.

Young and Kinnaman also note that "Forty-two percent of Millennials say that, 'when a text or message comes in, I usually stop what I'm doing to check it.'"[3]

Today, our noise comes in a wide variety of forms.

Gadgets. Gadgets in and of themselves are not bad things. But they do have the potential to generate a lot of noise in our lives—if we allow them.

This one dimension of noise has easily multiplied the noise levels in our world one hundred fold in the last ten years. Our gadgets are everywhere, giving us access to almost anything, at any point in time, just as quickly as we can iden-tify what we're looking for.

Smart phones in particular have become like a third hand that we know even better than the back of our physical hands. They provide us access to people via phone, text message, e-mail, social media, and the sort. They give us access to our calendars, contacts, photos, videos, and anything we might want to find via the Internet. They allow us to check the weather, attempt to organize our life, and even access files we may have placed on particular sites.

But it's not just what we have access to that makes these little buggers such distractions—it's *when* it allows us access to all of these things. Twenty-four, seven. There seems to be no place that people won't attempt to utilize their smart phone to check-in, post a picture, leave a comment, or simply surf the endless amounts of information that awaits them online. With people or alone. In bed. In class. On the job. At a restaurant. In a movie. Driving. Walking. Studying. Playing.

This new little device has quickly become the single biggest distraction of our lives.

Music. I hesitate to put music on this list because so much of it is beautiful art that has the ability to connect with our souls and enliven our spirits. But the reality is that far too many of us use music as a noisy way to distract ourselves from the realities we face. We seek temporary refuge or instant inspiration in the message or music of a particular song or artist in an attempt to forget about our current situation or overcome our current set of circumstances—even if only for a moment.

Music, like our gadgets, has become a near constant companion. It plays anywhere and everywhere we might choose to take our gadgets. And then, even if we're someplace where it would be totally inappropriate to be jamming to our personal playlist (at least without putting in earbuds), we're likely to find music playing in the background—with the intention of distracting us. On an elevator. In a waiting room. In the dentist chair. In the grocery store.

It covers the silence that we find so stark and unfamiliar in our culture of noise.

TV and media outlets. We are a culture that has quickly become obsessed with a multitude of screens. But our TVs and various media outlets have long been the cultural leaders in this regard. With the simple push of a button we can flip from the game to the news, from a sitcom to a made-for-television movie, from a reality show to a PBS classic. And then, depending on our cable or satellite setup, we can have a dozen or more variations on each of these genres—and more!

And with advancements in technology, we're now able to access any of these things from almost anywhere we can get a signal. First thing in the morning, on the go, in between classes, waiting to grab dinner with a friend, while eating dinner with a friend, and well into the late hours of the night.

These outlets bombard us with uncountable messages all in the same instant. From what to think about war, religion, politics, and the hottest issues of the day, to where to eat and what to wear for our next date, to what brands we should be seen with, or in, or eating, to what is (or should be) the new social norm for our ever-evolving North American culture.

I don't know that we've ever really considered what we mentally consume, and how it affects us, through these outlets. Regardless of whether we have or not—there are plenty of folks behind the curtain that have thought long and hard about the messages they're sending us—and most count on us not realizing that it's happening.

Social media. Even newer than most of our gadgets, social media may soon prove to be the noisiest distracter of them all. A place where everyone comes to share—well, everything. From their inner-most secrets to what they had for dinner last night, social media has become a literal mind-dump where one must intentionally sift through a lot of nonsense to find any nuggets or pearls that may or may not be present in these spaces.

And that's where "they" get us. The promise of the pearls or nuggets. We believe they're there—somewhere. And so we'll search—or more so, meander—through update upon update. We want to be encouraged, inspired, or simply in the know. We hope to find something worthy of liking or re-sharing—to let the iWorld know that we approve, and therefore exist. In what can feel like the blink of an eye, we can waste ninety minutes mindlessly roaming the same social media site, with little if anything to show for our time.

Then, of course, there are the ethics of most social media sites. Or, more accurately put, the ethics of the social media users of the different sites. How many people are projecting a different image of themselves than is true in reality? How many of them are making themselves out to sound much better than they really are—and why? How many of them are making things sound worse than they really are? How many people are using these cyber spaces as a place to attack others, spew hatred, or stalk unknowing potential victims? How many people are simply oversharing things that should never really be shared in the realm of social media?

And how, then, do we respond? What do we share? How accurately do we portray ourselves and our current life circumstances? What's our motivation for sharing at all?

So. Much. Noise.

The Noise of Those We Surround Ourselves With

Have you ever stopped to consider *who* you choose to surround yourself with—and why? The *friends* you choose, the *voices* that you allow to have agency or voice in your life, all serve to shape you in one way or another.

During most of your growing-up years, the shaping voices of your life were probably less of a conscious choice, and more of a natural outcome of the family you grew up in, the priorities of your parents, the kids in your neighborhood, the teachers you had at school and church, and then, eventually, the friends that you chose.

College is different. In many ways it's a season of life when the slate is wiped clear and you are given the opportunity to choose for yourself a whole new set of friends, teachers, pastors, and mentors. Aside from the roommate that you might get matched up with during the fall term of your first year on campus, there are a lot of choices you have in this regard. Of course, there's always the chance that you'll default to those people around you that are most present, most like you, most available, or quite simply the loudest.

But here's what you need to beware of. The people that you surround yourself with come with their own set of influential voices and noises and built-in distractions that serve to shape their lives. Just like you, each of these individuals—whether they are your peers, professors, employers, coaches, mentors, or someone else—all have experienced the world in their own unique ways that have caused them to be shaped and formed into the people that they are right now.

Their noise impacts you.

And *your* noise impacts them.

The Noise We Contribute

Yes, of course, we are all guilty of being contributors to the noise in our world. Every word spoken, every tweet posted, we are all leaving our own noise imprint on the world—every second of every day.

And while we don't have much control over the noise that other people contribute, we do have control over most of the noise that we put forth at any given moment.

Now don't get me wrong. I'm not advocating for a complete vow of silence, an abstinence of voice, or a total withdrawal from contributing to the mix and mash-up of everyday life.

What I am advocating for, however, is a more acute awareness of the noise of our world, our roles as contributors to the noise, and a more intentional way of living and contributing to such a noisy culture.

For too long, I believe, we've followed the lead of the world that has told us, "If you want to be heard, or if you want to make a difference, if you want to get your point across, or if you want to win the argument of the day, then you have to be the loudest and most persuasive voice out there. You have to become a *controller* of the noise, not just a *contributor*." And so, at whatever level we've understood this message, we've attempted to make a place for our own noise-making amidst a growing roar of noise that borders on deafening.

In choosing how we might contribute to the world—how we might shape the world—most of us have unknowingly opted to be a part of the problem, instead of a solution.

Why We Are Drawn Toward the Noise

I believe we are drawn toward noise because we fear what we might encounter in the silence.

Think about it.

When's the last time you opted to *limit* the noise in your life? When's the last time you chose to sit in silence instead of turning on music or the TV? When's the last time you chose to sit and listen to others speak—such that you could really hear what they were saying—as opposed to feeling compelled to jump in with your own ideas and opinions? When's the last time you trusted your instincts, or the still, small voice of God within you, instead of seeking the popular opinion of those who surround you?

On one level I think we believe that if we're not making noise, if we're not adding our voice to the mix and malaise of our noisy culture, then it's as if we don't exist—we don't matter. We all need to believe that our lives matter. That they count. That we count for something. That we're not some cosmic mistake, but that God has truly created us the way that we are for some reason, and that we have something meaningful to contribute to the world.

That leads us to a bigger reason I think we are drawn toward the noise in our world—we fear what we might encounter in the silence as it relates to God. We fear that if our inner and outer worlds get quiet enough we might indeed hear the still, small voice of God—and I think most of us are afraid of what we might hear in that space. Even worse, we fear that in that quiet place we won't actually hear anything at all. We'll go looking for God and we won't be able to find him—at least not in the ways we think we should. Dallas Willard expressed this very fear in these words, "But silence is frightening because it strips us as nothing else does, throwing us upon the stark realities of our life. It reminds us of death, which will cut us off from this world and leave only us and God. And in that quiet, what if there turns out to be very little to 'just us and God'?"[4]

So rather than bravely go looking for God, and a different way of living and being in the world, we opt for the noise—and all the distractions of this life—because it's what we see so readily modeled and prioritized all around us. It is our normal—and we don't even know it.

What do you think?

Does that seem fair? Does it sound accurate?

How a Noisy Culture Is Impacting Us

The noise we make, the noise we surround ourselves with, and the noise we are subjected to as members of the human race in our twenty-first-century world are all having an impact on us. We live distracted lives. We have learned how to exist in a noisy world. We even turn to noise as a form of self-medication and escape. We are being distracted from the things in life that are most important—the things of God.

I think we have moments when we are more acutely aware of the impact this distracted kind of existence is having on us. We sense that our world is not as it should be. Or maybe it's more so that we hope there's more to this life that we're living. We don't want to believe that this is it. That it's all really just about enduring a noisy world and grasping for a way to be heard—to be valued. Or hiding in the noise of this world so that we don't have to deal with our reality. Or even that we would opt for the distraction that noise provides because we fear what we might encounter in the absence of noise.

What Are We Missing?

The truth is, we are indeed missing out on much of the goodness and richness of life when we allow ourselves to be distracted by the noise of this world.

It is possible to experience beauty and peace, but it requires a way of life that is counter to our culture. It does not necessitate that we withdraw from our culture, or rage against it, but that we find ways to live more intentionally—more purposefully—within it.

But to truly engage this countercultural way of life will require that we learn some new skills, some new ways of pursuing and experiencing God, such that we are better able to control or manage the noise in our world.

We must learn and begin to practice the discipline of silence.

CHAPTER TWO

Silence

The LORD is in his holy temple;
let all the earth be silent before him.
—Habakkuk 2:20

There is a time for everything,
and a season for every activity under the heavens:
a time to be silent and a time to speak.
—Ecclesiastes 3:1, 7b

Silence is the discipline by which
the inner fire of God is tended and kept alive.
—Henri J. M. Nouwen, *The Way of the Heart*

Author Gary Holloway once wrote, "Silence is not our attempt to be spiritual or create spiritual experiences. Instead, it is an act of pure faith. We trust that God blesses those who spend time with him. We believe, even when we do not see, that God is working in us in the silence."[1]

My first attempts at silence made me feel like I had ADHD, or like I was a four-year-old—or maybe like I was a four-year-old with ADHD. There was something that felt very unnatural about attempting to be silent in our noisy culture.

And this should tell us something about both our culture and ourselves. If silence is the place—the fertile ground where God desires to meet us and work within us—then our noisy culture is in direct conflict with this need and our tendencies toward noise are in direct conflict with our desire to truly know God.

But if "only silence will allow us life-transforming concentration upon God,"[2] then we cannot afford to attempt a With-God kind of life without it. We must believe silence to be an utter necessity for experiencing God and hearing his still, small voice. We will need to make serious attempts to temper the noise of our world in order to more intentionally and persistently pursue the One True God.

But what does it mean to be silent? What is silence, really? And how is it that we might put ourselves in a position to have an encounter with God as we attempt to reduce or eliminate the noise in our lives? Well, I think it happens in a variety of ways.

An Outer Silence

A part of the discipline of silence is a definitive attempt to reduce the amount of external noise that surrounds us. It's a reduction of distractions. It is a literal creating of space for God to move more easily and readily in our presence. Not that he couldn't or doesn't already without this effort on our part. But this effort has more to do with us than it does God. We need the space. We need the distractions eliminated. We need the volume turned down so that we might better be able to see and hear God when he chooses to move and speak and lead. American writer and philosopher Rufus M. Jones said, "Silence itself, of course, has no magic. It may be sheer emptiness, absence of words or noise or music. It may be an occasion for slumber, or it may be a dead form. But it may be an intensified pause, a vitalized hush, a creative quiet, an actual moment of mutual and reciprocal correspondence with God."[3]

So outer silence becomes the place where we tell most of the noise that pollutes our days and our nights that we are choosing something different—something better. It's not that we're leaving the world, but that we're opting to turn down its volume for a time so that we might better tune in to what God is doing and how God is leading.

As we practice this kind of outer silence, God will begin to help us see much of the noise in our world for what it really is. He'll help us to better discern how best to manage, or even eliminate, many of the noisemakers that are only serving to distract us from what is good and beautiful and holy.

An Inner Silence

Even more important than an outer silence is an inner silence. Outer silence does us little good if we are not able to turn down the volume within.

American writer and theologian Frederick Buechner once wrote, "What deadens us most to God's presence within, I think, is the inner dialogue that we are engaged in within ourselves, the endless chatter of human thought. I suspect that there is nothing more crucial to true spiritual comfort than being able from time to time to stop that chatter, including the chatter of spoken prayer."[4]

The endless chatter of human thought. Our inner dialogue. It can all take on so many different forms. More often than not it probably revolves around our fears, insecurities, and anxieties about *who* we are, *how* we are, or *what* we are or are not doing in the world—and how that is being perceived by those around us. Instead of listening for the inner voice of God, we are distracted by the chatter that causes us to believe that we are not good enough, not smart enough, not holy enough, and not lovable enough. In many respects, it's like a series of harmful, hateful messages that have been recorded and put on a loop—causing us to become obsessed with our own shortcomings and struggles—and unable to identify the truth among the lies.

Learning to quiet the chatter (even the spoken prayer) enables us to hear, learn, distinguish, and discern God's voice without competition. If we are unfamiliar with his voice, we need to learn it. This is one of the reasons we so often struggle to know God's will, or discern if God is speaking to us. We don't trust what we think might be his leading in those moments of big questions or important decisions because we've not encountered his voice enough to be able to distinguish it from any of the other voices we might hear.

And it's not just that we can better hear from God in the midst of the silence, but that we can better associate God with the peace and grace and stillness that we also find when we quiet the inner chatter and engage in the practice of silence.

Listening

As we begin to reign in the noise in our outer and inner worlds, we often find that our own voice needs to be tamed as well.

Dallas Willard once wrote, "God gave us two ears and one mouth, it's been said, so that we might listen twice as much as we talk, but even that proportion is far too high on the side of talking."[5] Silence is not just about not talking, but learning how to listen as well. Really listen.

Far too often our conversations consist of two or more people half-heartedly listening to whoever happens to be talking at the time, only as much as it can inform the clever response or retort that we are contriving in our head.

James told us that we should be, "quick to listen, slow to speak and slow to become angry" (1:19). What a combination! It's like a one-two-three punch. And how opposite is this from what we typically see in our culture? Like most things we encounter in the Bible, this is a call to be counter to what we see and experience in the culture. I mean, how different would our world be if *everyone* were quick to listen. And upon taking time to really listen to others, what if we were truly slow to speak—because we were taking the time to appropriately process everything we had just heard? I can only imagine that if we were practicing these two things that much of the anger we experience in the world might disappear overnight.

In silence we are freed of our need to be heard. Or to have something to say. Or to be thought of at all. In silence, we connect with God and better understand the degree to which we are known and loved and defined by him such that we don't feel compelled to have something noble or notable to say. This freedom then allows us to be more fully present to others—and to God.

Learning to listen requires learning to exercise our self-control—another characteristic (not to mention, fruit of the Spirit) that seems to be seldom modeled in our noisy world of entitlement and impulse.

Control

Gary Holloway wrote, "The purpose of silence is not merely to rest from the noise around us. It is not primarily a way to detach ourselves from our worries and distractions. Instead, in silence we are reattaching ourselves to the Source of our lives."[6] Some might think that the choice of silence is a choice of passivity and non-participation in the world and in one's own life. But in a sense it's the exact opposite. A decision to engage in the practice of silence is to bring oneself—one's thoughts, words, and behavior—under control and into the submission of the Lord's leading.

The apostle Paul used vivid imagery to make this same point to the young Christians in Corinth when he said:

> Do you not know that in a race all the runners run, but only one gets the prize? Run in such a way as to get the prize. Everyone who competes in the games goes into strict training. They do it to get a crown that will not last, but we do it to get a crown that will last forever. Therefore I do not run like someone running aimlessly; I do not fight like a boxer beating the air. No, I strike a blow to my body and make it my slave so that after I have preached to others, I myself will not be disqualified for the prize. (1 Cor. 9:24–27)

Our thoughts. One of the ways that silence leads to this kind of control is in our mind—and the things we think about. I don't know if you've ever noticed, but our minds have a way of getting us into trouble. Paul said that we must "take captive every thought to make it obedient to Christ" (2 Cor. 10:5). But too often we fail to take Paul's advice.

Whether we let ourselves fantasize on certain images or people, or allow ourselves to get worked up over a multitude of possible scenarios about the immediate or distant future that run through our head, or even in the incessant mental replaying of past experiences—one of the ways we express our hope, faith, and love in God is by taking control of our thought life. It requires the daily, hourly, and even minute-to-minute kind of training that Paul described in the 1 Corinthians 9 passage.

If we aren't able to bring our thoughts under control, then we'll likely have little chance of learning to control any other area of our life.

Our words. In considering why it is we might need to control our words, we look to the book of James, the brother of Jesus and one of the church's early pastors, when he explains:

> We all stumble in many ways. Anyone who is never at fault in what they say is perfect, able to keep their whole body in check.
>
> When we put bits into the mouths of horses to make them obey us, we can turn the whole animal. Or take ships as an example. Although they are so large and are driven by strong winds, they are steered by a very small rudder wherever the pilot wants to go. Likewise, the tongue is a small part of the body, but it makes great boasts. Consider what a great forest is set on fire by a small spark. The tongue also is a fire, a world of evil among the parts of the body. It corrupts the whole body, sets the whole course of one's life on fire, and is itself set on fire by hell.
>
> All kinds of animals, birds, reptiles and sea creatures are being tamed and have been tamed by mankind, but no human being can tame the tongue. It is a restless evil, full of deadly poison.
>
> With the tongue we praise our Lord and Father, and with it we curse human beings, who have been made

in God's likeness. Out of the same mouth come praise and cursing. My brothers and sisters, this should not be. Can both fresh water and salt water flow from the same spring? My brothers and sisters, can a fig tree bear olives, or a grapevine bear figs? Neither can a salt spring produce fresh water. (James 3:2–12)

Words are powerful. They have the capacity to encourage and uplift, or tear down and destroy. James likened the tongue to bits in the mouth of a horse, or a rudder on a ship. It is powerful and will ultimately serve to direct the path of our life. To lack control of this small and seemingly insignificant thing would be a grand mistake. Whether carelessly spoken or craftily written, whether shared with a single individual or via social media to the masses, our words need to be put forth slowly—with forethought and intention.

We would all be served well to let our words be few.

Our behavior. Our behavior is the natural outflow of what we think and what we speak. Where our mind dwells tends to set a trajectory for our life. What we speak tends to dictate our course of action. So naturally, our behavior is the means by which we'll get to our destination—chosen or quite by accident.

Do we know where we're going? If we've not made this connection between our thoughts, words, and behavior— and our need to control these things—then we're not likely to have a clue of where we are heading.

We cannot make the mistake of simply addressing our behavior though, or we might be tricked into believing that we are dealing with the entirety of the noise, without really getting to its root. This is the same line of action that leads us to sin management. When one attempts to deal with only the sinful behavior (like looking at porn), instead of searching for the root of the sin problem (for example, why one might feel drawn to look at porn), any fix is only temporary because we're dealing with what is obvious and seen but not dealing with the problem behind the problem. It's the difference between mowing over a weed and pulling it up roots and all. A weed that is mown over will likely be back, even bigger and stronger than before, because its root system has continued to grow beneath the surface. But a weed that is pulled up, including the root system, is eliminated from the lawn.

As we've previously acknowledged, we cannot do all of the work required to experience God and grow in our faith. We are only a part of this mysterious equation. But we do play a role. And learning to be self-controlled, with the grace and assistance of God's Spirit, is a big part of the work we do every time we practice the discipline of silence.

Losing Control

And although we've just talked about how silence brings control to certain areas of our life, we must recognize that silence is an absolute relinquishing of control at the exact same time.

In his book, *Invitation to a Journey*, author and theologian Robert Mulholland explained that "silence is the inner act of letting go."[7] While we are attempting to reign in the wily ways of our thoughts, words, and deeds, we are at the same time learning how to give up control of the outcome— or how God might choose to work in us and through us as we engage in the practice of silence.

This is one of the biggest tensions—the fact that any given discipline will not consistently yield a desired outcome. Remember, the spiritual disciplines are not a magic formula for getting God to do (or give us) what we want. The disciplines are not about God, other than the fact that the intended result will bring us deeper into the With-God life. No, the disciplines are really about us. They are about putting us in a position where we will be less distracted by the noise of our world and, therefore, better able to connect to and commune with the Living God. "Therefore, in silence we receive from God. We receive deep peace. We receive strength for the day. We receive patience to wait for God to work."[8]

This is the work of silence in our life.

CHAPTER THREE

Learning to Quiet Our Inner (and Outer) World

Upon learning that there are avenues and pathways by which we might better experience God and grow more intentionally in our relationship with him, our natural instinct might be to dive in headfirst. If silence is one of those pathways, then why not schedule a silent retreat and prepare to be blown away by what we experience in twenty-four or forty-eight hours of quiet?

Well, for starters, we would probably find it so radically uncomfortable and jarring to our system that we would flee from it within the first twenty-four to forty-eight minutes with no desire to ever return to it. And it's not just that it's so foreign to our system, but as we attempt to remove many of the noises in our life we are likely to become acutely aware of the things that we have been suppressing, unaware of, or only beginning to struggle with, making our challenges in silence now two or three or tenfold.

Why We Can't Jump into the Deep End

Spiritual muscles, much like our physical muscles, take time to develop. Similarly, we are not born with the ability to dive into a body of water and swim. Countless deaths are reported every year of non-swimmers who venture too far out into lakes or rivers and get into trouble. We even hear stories of experienced swimmers getting into trouble and drowning.

It's important for us to learn the basics of the different spiritual disciplines before we plunge ourselves into the depths of the With-God life. Learning the basics can help to ensure that we have a growing working knowledge of what we're doing so that we're less likely to get distracted by the practice itself or overwhelmed by where the experience is leading us.

Taking time to learn as we go, and being intentional in our practice of the spiritual disciplines, will help us to become well-trained disciples and not people who simply look to gorge on spiritual experiences.

The Challenge of Going Slow

But that's a problem. We don't like to go slow, do we? We don't like to be a beginner. Once we identify something that we don't know, but want to know (or something we aren't good at that we want to be good at), we tend to want to do whatever it takes to quickly become proficient in it, if not a master of it.

Why do we do this? Because we live in a society of instant gratification. We want what we want and we want it now. We don't know how to wait because we aren't accustomed to having to do so. We live in a consumerist culture that caters to our every whim and perceived need—which includes not *wasting* time waiting. As we've come to learn that we do not have to wait for most things in life, we've lost the capacity to wait, while also losing our ability to see the value of what can come in the waiting.

But wait we must.

The spiritual disciplines do not provide instant results. Nor can they be quickly learned, fully understood, or ever really mastered. And that goes against everything we've come to believe about this life. We've been raised to believe that if we want it bad enough, and if we work hard enough, we can achieve almost anything. But this is not true of the disciplines. No matter how long we practice different spiritual disciplines, we will never work our way into a mastery of them.

Author and Christian spiritualist Thomas Merton, when describing the practice of spiritual disciplines, once wrote, "We do not want to be beginners. But let us be convinced of the fact that we will never be anything else but beginners, all our life."[1] Yet another challenging truth on our journey toward discovering more sacred pathways to God.

What Might It Look Like to Begin to Practice Silence?

What are some simple ways, some smaller ways, some slower ways of beginning to engage and practice the discipline of silence? Here are just a few that you might consider. There's no need to incorporate all of these ideas at the same time.

Remember, you're just a beginner, but it is definitely possible to incorporate more than one of these practices into your early engagement and exploration of the discipline of silence.

Get up early. Getting up early is a great way to experience the natural silence that comes from being awake while most of the world around us is still quiet and asleep. In the darkness and in the stillness and in the quiet of the early morning hours, as you are still trying to wake up, you'll find that you are much more likely to be unencumbered by the noise and worries that normally fill your day. In this quiet time there's very little you need to do to create silence, and so you're given more of an opportunity to enjoy it and to experience the peace and holy that can be found there.

Go somewhere quiet. Another option is to go and find a quiet place. Living on campus, or living with roommates, can often make it hard (if not impossible) to experience silence where you live. But in all likelihood, you would not have to travel far to get off campus and into a relatively quiet place where the outer noise of the world will be hushed, and your opportunity to commune with God in silence is made easier.

Be still. Another great way to engage the practice of the discipline of silence is to simply be still. Learning to be still is something you can do regardless of where you are or what's going on around you. Learning to be still is a way of quieting your body and learning that when your body calms down, your mind and heart are likely to slow down as well. And in the stillness you create space for God to speak and have his way in your life.

Be quiet. It seems obvious enough, but actually closing your mouth and learning to be quiet is an essential part of engaging in the practice of silence. What would it look like for you to go fifteen minutes without speaking? How about thirty? Might this be a good way for you to engage this discipline of silence? By quieting your mouth and controlling your words, you are giving your mind the chance to slow down and quiet itself, again giving God space in your interior world.

Turn off your phone. This might be one of the hardest ideas for this generation of students to get on board with. Your phone is probably one of the single biggest distractions in your life, and one of the largest contributors of noise in your world. What would it look like for you to turn that off for thirty minutes or for an hour? How about a day? Seeing this as a major need in our current culture, some leaders have begun to refer to this kind of practice as a digital Sabbath, where you turn off your devices and unplug from your technologies for a predetermined amount of time so that they will not be a distraction.

Stay off of the Internet. Similarly, how might you create more space for God in your life if you were to choose to stay off of the Internet for an afternoon or evening or weekend? How many of your struggles might be thwarted, or rendered altogether inconsequential, by staying off of the Internet for some time? How might this act free up more time and space in your life, and reduce the amount of noise in your world, allowing God to more easily get your attention and speak to your heart?

Don't turn on the TV. The television is another contributor to the noise of our world. It can distract us in half-hour or hour-long blocks of time, and can even serve to distract us for several hours in any given day. What would it look like for you to unplug your TV for a day or a few days or even a week at a time? How might this one act reduce the volume of noise in your world and create more space for God?

Listen for your inner chatter. This idea might take a little more time, and a little more effort, than the ones we've explored so far, because it's not as simple as going someplace or hitting the off button. This particular exercise will require that you become more aware of the noise and inner dialogue happening within you.

To assist in this process, it might be worth having a journal available or somewhere you can jot down the items that seem so prevalent or pressing in your heart or mind. Once these items are written down, they will likely cease to distract you in the same fashion. When your mind sees that you have acknowledged the important issues racing about, it may very well begin to quiet down, believing that you now have a plan to address those items later on. Plus, taking a moment to write these things down will indeed give you a better idea as to the kinds of things that regularly consume your mind and weigh on your heart.

Pay close attention to your words. Similar to being quiet, the practice of paying attention to your words should help you to be slower to speak and more intentional and thoughtful with the words that you choose to speak. This will help you to stop talking for the sake of being heard, the sake of being seen, and the sake of being valued, because you won't associate your words with your worth. When you challenge yourself to pay closer attention to what you say, and why you say it, you will be encouraged to make the most of your words and more likely to speak less, ultimately creating more space for God.

Really listen to a friend. This is the practice that will probably gain you the most attention and favor with your friends. Everyone wants to be heard. When we choose to become a listener, a *good* listener, we give other people the gift of being heard. When we begin to really listen to others, we bless them because we give them something that is very rare in our noisy culture today—the undivided and undistracted focus that everyone deserves. In this, you create space for God to not only work in your midst but in the midst of others as well.

How Might You Know If It's Working?

Another one of the challenging aspects of practicing spiritual disciplines is the fact that it can be hard to tell when (or if) anything is happening. Let us mirror this against the backdrop of a new runner or dieter looking to lose weight. One can begin to reorder their life to include new exercise routines, eating plans, and sleep schedules and notice—well, not much. There might be the physical discomfort of working out muscles that have not been worked out, hunger pains or cravings from withholding certain kinds of food from the body, and even some social challenges from giving more attention to when you go to sleep.

But true results can feel elusive in the beginning.

We know we're doing work. But we're not seeing any of the results we were anticipating. The same challenge can exist with our practice of the spiritual disciplines.

And yet, I believe there are some signs, some indicators, which we might indeed notice as we engage in the sacred practice of silence.

A noticeable quiet. An obvious change will be a quieter life. Once we become aware of the volume at which we've been living life, and experience some quieter spaces and places, we might begin to eliminate some of the noisier distractions from our life without even noticing it. This, of course, assumes that we are choosing to no longer use noise to distract ourselves, or as a place to hide from different elements of life that we would rather avoid.

An inner peace. When we take steps to turn down the volume in our life, and experience some of the richness and blessing that can be found in these new quiet spaces, it can kindle within us a peace that has not had room to exist. Like a smoldering pile of leaves and twigs that has once been suffocated by too many other things, this inner peace can ignite and begin to fan into flame once provided with enough time and space through the practice of silence.

A stronger sense of connection to the Holy. As we prove consistent in our attempts to keep the noise levels of our life at a minimum, we will be consistently reminded of why we're doing it, directing our thoughts and our gaze to the One True God. This kind of consistent attention will undoubtedly grow our awareness of, and affection for, God in our life. As we sense this connection happening, and strengthening (although we're not quite sure how), we will be encouraged to keep at it.

And there could easily be other signs that you could identify as you begin to consistently engage in the practice of silence. The challenge is not to presume you know what results should look like.

The Need to Be Consistent and Persistent

One of the other challenges that we encounter in our practice of spiritual disciplines is a willingness and ability to be in it for the long haul. The With-God life is not a sprint, but much more like a marathon. But I don't think marathon even captures it accurately, because marathons have finish lines. The spiritual life is definitely more like a marathon than it is a sprint, and marathons require consistency and persistence in order to run the race well.

Consistency is simply the willingness to show up with great regularity. You don't have to be engaged in the practice every single day—because we wouldn't want to trick ourselves into thinking that we could earn our way into anything. But it does mean that we're showing up with great regularity such that our spiritual muscles are getting readily worked, and subsequently growing in all the right ways and not weakening or shrinking.

Persistence is when we choose to stick with it even when things get tough. It is important to remember that we have an Enemy, an Adversary, who will try to distract us, discourage us, and do whatever he can to keep us from investing in our relationship with God. Persistence is the runner who hits the wall, and keeps running, believing that the pain will soon pass. It's the athlete who, despite the wind, or rain, or cold, chooses to get outside and work. Persistence is believing (and hoping and trusting) that as we are faithful to do our part in this mysterious process of pursing God, that God will be faithful to honor those efforts—in some way, shape, or form.

We have a God who loves us and wants to do life with us. But he wants us to choose him—over and above the noise of our world. He won't compete with that noise. He wants us to deal with it—with his help. But make no mistake about it, he's waiting on us to make the choice.

CHAPTER FOUR

Hurry

Hurry is not just a disordered schedule.
Hurry is a disordered heart.
—John Ortberg, *The Life You've Always Wanted*

I f noise were the only distraction we were up against, we might have a fighting chance. But our Enemy knows this. He knows that in order to really hinder us he's going to have to get to us on multiple levels. So while he attempts to crank up the volume of our life, he's also tempting us to live life at breakneck speeds.

Just as noise can serve as a distraction that can drown out the still, small voice of God, hurry is a weapon that our Adversary can also use to keep us on the run—with little (if any) time to squeeze God in.

But God doesn't want to be squeezed into our lives. He desires to be at the center of it. He did, after all, create us and bless us with the lives that we have. And although he's not content to sit on the sidelines and wait for us to call his number, he will not force his way into our hurried existence.

He wants us to want him. He wants us to want him enough that we'll rearrange our frenetically paced lives in order to choose a different pace. A less hurried pace. A pace that allows God time and space to speak and be heard.

A Culture of Hurry

We live in a world obsessed with speed. We like things fast, but we love things faster than fast. Many of the advances we see in technology have to do with doing things faster. We want our food fast. We want our games, apps, and shows downloaded fast. We want updates on the game, on breaking news around the world, and on what our friends had for dinner all in the same moment.

If possible, we'll often opt to do multiple things at the same time—believing that somehow we are getting them done quicker—and thereby giving ourselves more time . . . to fit in more things.

And this kind of life, this kind of pace, is both modeled by most of the leaders we encounter and upheld by society at large as a sign of intelligence and significance. *If you're not busy then you must not be that great.* Because if you were great, everyone would want you to be involved in everything—and of course, you would have to oblige. Because that's what awesome people do. They fill up their calendars and hurry from appointment to appointment with barely a moment to catch their breath, let alone take an intentional moment to slow down and sit down and simply be still.

In a culture of hurry, slowing down and resting is often seen as a sign of weakness. So we live a life of survival of the fittest—or in this case, the fastest.

A Campus of Opportunity

Not only do we live in a culture obsessed with speed, but you are likely a part of a campus community that offers an unlimited number of opportunities to get involved, both in and outside of the classroom.

Understanding the consumeristic nature of our culture, as well as the significance and challenge of retaining students, more and more colleges and universities are packing the campus calendar with opportunity upon opportunity for students to participate in. The hope is that every single student will find some place to fit in, contribute, and belong—and in doing so end up remaining a part of the campus community for the duration of their college years.

And that's not a bad thing. In fact, there is much that is good and noble about this way of thinking and operating as an institution.

However, what I have found to be more true to experience is that the students who would have struggled to get involved when the opportunities were less bountiful, still tend to opt out of getting involved when they are more bountiful. And those students who would have chosen to get involved if there was only a single event over the course of an entire week, are now finding themselves with limitless options for filling their co-curricular calendar. And with a culture that encourages and celebrates the hurried life—we seem to have more and more students choosing this kind of frenzied existence.

A Slave to the Calendar

When I was a college student back in the mid-90s, planners were the way that organized students attempted to stay on top of everything they had to do. I didn't know many who used these kinds of calendars, other than to maybe keep their assignment due dates in front of them. But even that seemed to be a small minority of students that tended to lean toward the extreme end of organization and being overly obsessed about the possibility of missing one of those important deadlines.

Today, it seems that most students I know utilize some online calendar system that can easily be synced between multiple devices—and it's not for show, but out of total necessity. Many of the students I encounter on campus these days tend to be involved and committed to an extreme. These students have little (if any) noticeable margin in their lives. They simply run from one thing to the next.

The college years are designed to be some of the most flexible and fluid of life. As college students, you will have more control over the entirety of your schedule than at any other point in your life. But flexibility and fluidity are not what I see in the lives of most college students today.

Instead, I see students who are driven like slaves—by a calendar of their own creation. They live frenzied, rushed, unenjoyable lives—all for the sake of what?

The answer is different from one student to the next, but in almost every instance there is an undercurrent of uncertainty and even fear.

FOMO

FOMO. Is that still a thing?

FOMO stands for "fear of missing out." Regardless of whether or not it's still a phrase that today's students are using, it is a reality that drives many of the decisions that young people make in regard to their schedules and pace of life.

There are so many good things, so many great things, to be involved in that the best one can hope to do is to cram as many of these opportunities into their twenty-four-hour day with the hope that they don't somehow miss out on the one thing that everyone else will be talking about on the following day.

But it's not just the social scene that is causing students to fear that they might miss out. It's the perfect internship that just might set you up for the job of your dreams upon graduation. And if you can't discern which one is the perfect internship, well, then you'd better take all three.

There's also the study groups. Yes, they often come in multiples as well, because the optimal study group cannot be too large. And there are different study groups that meet different needs. There is, of course, the study group with the few students who seem to know everything there is to know about the subject at hand. This gathering is a must. But there's also the study group that has that really cute guy or girl that you'd like to make time for, but just can't seem to find the time. So why not hit up a second study group where you can maximize your time—covering the subject matter again while also getting to spend some quality time with that special someone. And that's just for one of your three, or four, or more classes.

Did someone say classes? Oh, that's right. That's why you're at college in the first place, right? You're stacking your schedule and trying to make it all work so that you can fit it all in—and graduate on time. But if one major is good, a double major is probably twice as good. And a minor would allow you to explore that area that you think you might have some interest in—so why not add that as well. What's a few more classes each term anyway?

And with the outrageous costs of higher education, and the compulsion to keep up with your peers, and therefore live above your means, a job is almost an absolute necessity for many students. But in an attempt to get the optimal number of hours, and still be a part of everything happening everywhere else, some students will choose to take on a second or third job just so they can get the kind of work calendar that will earn them enough money while at the same time not cause them to miss out on anything.

Tempted To Do It All

The temptation that I see all too many students dealing with is the temptation to do it all. They want to be everywhere, and do everything, and meet everyone. They don't want to let anyone down or leave anyone out. They want to have their cake and eat it too . . . and then some. They load up their calendars and set out at an unsustainable pace, believing that somehow they will be able to do it all, and that it will yield—something.

But what I see far too often is a crash somewhere along the way. Students attempting to live these full, frenzied lives eventually run out of gas, and while coasting on the fumes that remain, they desperately try to fit in just a few more things, before eventually screeching to a complete halt.

It may start with feelings of strain within important relationships, or missed meetings, and eventually a major let down or failure. But ultimately, it will be a student's free-falling GPA that gets their attention. Much like the indicator light that goes off in your car when your gas tank gets low, the grades are often the only indicator that will get a student's attention that they are headed toward a fatal end. Sure, many students will choose to ignore that warning indicator for as long as they possibly can, but it does eventually get their attention. By then, however, it's often too late. In a last-ditch effort to salvage their GPA, or simply keep from failing out, these students will abandon everything that they are involved in outside of the classroom and spend the remaining weeks of the term trying to dig themselves out of the academic hole they have created.

But with little left in their gas tank, this is a task that proves to be much harder than they might have guessed.

So why does this happen?

What You Don't Know

One of the reasons I think so many students today overfill their lives and hurry around, day after day, from commitment to commitment, is simply because they don't know what they want. They don't know what they're looking for.

There's something internal that has alerted you to the significance of these college years—and that they're years that will serve to shape the trajectory of your life for many years to come. You sense this, but still don't know how it's supposed to inform your present life decisions.

And the Enemy knows that in these moments of not knowing you feel tempted to let your foot off the gas pedal and look to God for answers. So rather than allow that to happen, he sets out to convince you that your answers will be found in adding a little more of this or that to your life.

Obsessed with Trying to Figure It Out

Up to this point in your life, much of what has defined happiness for you has had to do with having your needs met. It's not just you—we're all like that. We want to be comfortable, we want to be safe, and we want to be secure. We want people to like us and like what we do. We want these things until we're awakened to the fact that we're not the center of the universe. God is.

Frederick Buechner once wrote, "The place God calls you to is the place where your deep gladness and the world's deep hunger meet."[1] This doesn't sound much like a life of self-centered self-indulgence. This doesn't sound like racing around, attempting to try every last trick or fad, with the hope of squeezing out even an ounce of joy, or peace, or momentary contentment.

According to Buechner, there is a place, a sweet spot, where God might want us to arrive—an intersection where our deep gladness and the world's deep hunger come together. But if this place sounds magical and mystical and far from our reality, it's because we've never slowed down long enough to learn what our gifts, talents, or passions are. We may have caught some glimpses here and there that have alluded to these things, but that's only because God has hardwired them within us. The fact that we've only caught glimpses of these things should clue us in to just how cunning and deceptive our Adversary can be.

If we ever hope to identify and better understand this hardwiring within, then we'd better learn how to deal with the hurry that so often keeps us overwhelmed and fearful of missing out on, well, everything; and learn how to create some time and space for God to begin to speak to us about such things.

And it's not just about you either. Buechner wrote of this intersection of our deep gladness meeting up with the world's deep need. God wants us to use our gifts to help people in need—a world in need. But that's not how the world teaches us to think about our purpose in the world, is it?

Defined by Work/Achievement

I am convinced that a part of our frenetic and frenzied compulsion with hurry has to do with a lack of understanding about what truly defines us. Our culture has long conveyed the message that what most defines us is the work that we do, the things we're able to achieve, and the accomplishments we can point to in our lives. We are conditioned to be doers and believe that our titles, pay grades, level of influence, and growing notoriety define us.

So we spend way too much of our time, energy, and attention focused on the things that we think will set us up for this kind of life. We fill our schedules with an overabundance of experiences and opportunities that we hope will move us in the right direction. But what we don't seem to understand in this season is that the full schedule and hurried pace we keep give us little chance of ever being able to understand our true purpose or identity, because we leave no space to be still in the presence of God.

What Are We Missing?

Just like the challenges we experience in the noise of our world, the hurried lives we lead are distracting us from experiencing the beauty and bounty of the With-God life.

There is a better way of living, but it necessitates that we look at our approach to life through a different set of lenses. We need to learn to see, and understand, the world as God does. We need to consider ways that we can live life that are counter to our culture. It means that we will need to call into question the paradigms and practices that have led us to this kind of existence.

And just as we had to learn some new ways of pursuing God and practicing ways of living that are counter to much of our world as it relates to noise, so we must with the hurry of our lives as well.

In this instance, we must learn and begin to practice the discipline of Sabbath.

CHAPTER FIVE

Sabbath (Slowing)

Be still, and know that I am God.
—Psalm 46:10

Jesus was often busy, but never hurried.
—John Ortberg, *The Life You've Always Wanted*

Sabbath frames our entire life, helping us set
priorities and determine which of our activities
and aspirations bring honor to God.
—Norman Wirzba, *Living the Sabbath*

I once had the pleasure of spending some time with a well-known author and thinker. I had read some of his books, learned from him in one of my seminary classes, and been challenged and inspired by him through a couple of public addresses.

Over the course of our day together, I eventually asked him about the breadth and depth of his work and all that it had taken to become such a well-respected and highly sought-after voice in the Christian world. What he shared surprised me.

He talked about the odd hours he kept. Having commitments on both coasts, he wanted to wake up in the morning as if he were a permanent resident on the east coast. When they were waking up, he wanted to wake up. But he also wanted to be up late with the folks on the west coast and interact with them as if he were a permanent resident there.

Surprised by how little sleep it sounded like he was getting, I joked about having an espresso drip hooked up to his arm as if it were an IV. He got a good laugh, but confirmed that there was almost always a pot of coffee on or a coffee run in his near future. But that wasn't what surprised me. What surprised me was what he said next.

"When I get to heaven I'm going to ask God about why he created sleep. I think it's a design flaw. Think about all of the work there is, and all that could be done, if we didn't have to mess with sleep." I about fell out of my chair.

I've heard of driven people before, but having the audacity to question God's design of human beings seemed more than extreme. Especially because I did not think he was joking. It appeared as though his life reflected his sentiments. But for someone as learned and faithful as I had previously known this man to be, my questions surrounding his understanding of Sabbath began to pile up.

In his heart and mind, he clearly saw Sabbath as a nuisance, if not a burden, and I cannot identify how (or if) it was something that he practiced.

The Gift of Rest

Sabbath was never meant to be a burden, but a blessing. It was modeled by God in the creation narrative in Genesis. It represents what God created after he created man. It's almost as if he knew we would not discover it or value it if he didn't include it as a part of creation. God uses the last day in the creation story to create peace and rest that honors him and serves to rejuvenate and reorient his created.

It's hard to know for sure if we were hardwired by God to want to rest or not. On one hand we believe that when God first created Adam and Eve that they were perfect and without sin. But, on the other, we also see that it is the day after he created Adam that he created a day for rest. And we see that later on in the story of God and the Israelites that Sabbath becomes one of the cornerstone elements of the covenant between them. Hardwired or not, it is clear that this idea of Sabbath was one that was to be taken seriously. Whether it was (or is) understood as a gift or not is another issue. But in its design, Sabbath is supposed to be a gift from God to his people that ultimately points us back to him.

Gary Holloway wrote, "what a loving God has done for his people through the ages is to give them another practice to help. The marvelous gift of Sabbath. A day when we give up our busy striving. A day of gentle rest."[1] The gift of rest can take on many different forms, but it is ultimately tied to the freedom it yields us.

Freedom from the need to perform. In a culture as driven as ours, and within the context of an academic system that has long valued achievement over and above learning, freedom from a need to perform is incredibly liberating. Of course we want to do our best in the things that we are called to be a part of. But this desire should stem from a desire to honor and glorify God, and not achieve the approval or praise of those around us.

Practicing Sabbath serves to free us from this perceived need to perform. It also helps to identify those around us who might be pushing or pressuring us to be overly concerned with appearances and perfection.

Freedom from the need to produce. Sabbath doesn't just free us from the need to perform, but the need to produce as well. Somewhere along the way effort was left by the wayside as something that was without value unless it yielded something.

But God doesn't care what we produce. Sure, he's created us with specific gifts, talents, and passions that he desires for us to use to help meet needs in the world. But he doesn't need us to produce anything essential to life. He can do that all well and good on his own. I think he chooses to include us because of how the *process* does a work in *us*. But a lot of the systems and structures that make up our North American culture do not uphold this same outlook on production.

Our educational system is a great example of this. In the first few years of elementary education there are two sets of grades—one describing the student's effort level and the other describing their actual achievement. But by the second or third grade the effort category of grading is removed from consideration and everything hinges on the achievement grade. Teaching at the college level, I see how years in this system serve to shape a student's approach to their college years. For most, it's simply *achieve the grade no matter the cost*. This rarely translates into steady and consistent commitment and dedication to the assignments and coursework of the class over the duration of the term. Instead, I tend to see a lot of overwhelmed students who struggle to prioritize their time and then relent to compromise (at a variety of levels) in order to do what they can to still pull out the desired grade.

God wants more for us. We are so much more than the sum total of what we produce. And we find this out through the consistent practice of Sabbath.

Freedom from the need to be all things. Practicing Sabbath also frees us from feeling overwhelmed by our perceived need to be all things. When we put our head down and go, go, go, it can be all too easy to ignore our gifts, lose sight of our passions, and simply do whatever we need to do in order to make things happen. We like when people lean on us and tell us they need us and, since we'd hate to let them down, we take on more and more in an attempt to be something magnificent. Rather than focus on a few things—and do them really well—we're likely to take on too many things and delve further into a hurried (and therefore increasingly futile) existence.

But Sabbath frees us from this compulsion, because the time and space that Sabbath requires of us creates an environment in which God can remind us of how he's made us, and why he's made us, and what he's made us for.

Freedom from the need to please all people. Finally, Sabbath frees us from the need to please all people. In Sabbath we are reminded of *who* we are and *whose* we are. As a beloved child of God, our identity is deeply rooted and secure, which should free us from the need to attain the approval of others. If we're doing what we believe God has called us to do, it won't matter if it's popular or not. If we're doing what we believe God wants us to do, we'll feel more confident when we meet resistance or opposition. When we're consistently practicing Sabbath, we're freed from our need to work for the praise of others, because we know that we have a God who is pleased with us in the ways we choose to honor him with our life.

Ultimately, this gift of rest is a divine invitation into the With-God life. It is a chance for us to put aside the hurried, frenzied, frantic ways of the world and rest in the fact that God is in control. God is our provider. God is God.

The Reminder of Rest

God is God—and we are not.

Seems pretty straightforward. But when you consider what it is we communicate in the hurried lives that we lead—to God, ourselves, and others—you get something . . . well, god-like. We consciously or subconsciously believe we are so important that to take time to rest, or even slow down, would feel like careless behavior. We believe, in our heart of hearts, that stopping or slowing down could potentially put all the things we've been busily giving ourselves to in jeopardy. We convince ourselves that we need to stay engaged because God needs us to so that things don't fall apart while we've got our heels kicked up—"resting."

Gary Holloway wrote, "On our Sabbath, we stop working to remind ourselves that it is God who provides."[2] We so badly need this reminder. At every phase of life, but especially during the formative college years. If you can grab hold of this truth—that God is God and we are not—then your outlook on life will be very different from the rest of the world. This truth serves to reorient us to the life that we lead, the people we encounter, and the purpose with which we approach everything. We need to be reminded, with great regularity, about the plans and purposes that God has for us and how best we can partner with him in order to fulfill those things.

The Significance of Slowing

Sabbath is not just about stopping, but about slowing down as well. When we think about Sabbath solely as stopping we're tempted to think about it like an on/off switch or a car with two gears. We're in one position or the other. We're stopped or we're off and running.

But I think a significant part of practicing Sabbath is the reorientation to the world that we experience. As we slow, or as we stop, or as we rest, we are awakened to the ways that God is working all around us, as well as how we might better come alongside him in the work he is doing. We're challenged to reenter the world of work with a different heart and mind. We are called to be more thoughtful and intentional—in every way—but especially with regard to the pace that we keep.

Slowing becomes a challenge to keep our gaze fixed on Jesus throughout the entirety of our work—no matter what our work might be. When we remove the on/off switch and replace it with a dimmer switch of sorts, we are challenged to pay closer (and more consistent) attention to where it is set. We need to be aware of those around us who might attempt to turn up the intensity. We need to be aware of our own tendencies to want to turn up the intensity—in the name of performance or production or a need to be all things to all people.

Slowing, and not just stopping, requires our constant attention to this area of life—and the challenges we face to maintain a more sustainable (not to mention God-honoring) pace of life.

It's Actually a Command

And then, of course, there's this: "Remember the Sabbath day by keeping it holy" (Exod. 20:8). Of all of the spiritual practices or spiritual disciplines that we might engage for the sake of pursuing and experiencing God, the consistent participation in Sabbath-keeping is the only one that is actually a command from God. Yes! A command.

When God was establishing his covenant with the Israelites, not long after their deliverance from Egyptian captivity, he gave them the Ten Commandments. They were to serve as a cornerstone for the Law that would instruct the Israelites on how to live the With-God life. Of the ten, the first four commandments had to do with the relationship between God and humans, and the other six had to do with the relationships between humans.

It was the fourth commandment—after 1) love God, 2) do not worship idols, and 3) do not take the name of the Lord in vain—that God then commanded, "Remember the Sabbath day by keeping it holy." Four key commands bringing shape to the With-God life and God chose to include a day of rest. With the primary purpose of honoring God, and reminding us that he is the one in control, the Sabbath was (and is) also intended as an opportunity for humans to rest from our normal rhythms and routines.

But this call to slow down, stop, and rest sounds much easier than it actually is. I know, because I consistently find myself in tension with God's call to practice Sabbath and the world's call to go, go, go. Yet, this is a good tension to have, for if we view the tension as a call to turn our gaze upon God (and not a dreadful Christian duty that we have to fulfill) we will be encouraged to enter into Sabbath for all that it has to offer.

Let's look at some practical steps for incorporating Sabbath into our hurried life.

CHAPTER SIX

Learning to Move with Greater Intention

Awareness is a funny thing. We're rarely aware of what we *are* aware of—and what we're *not* aware of. It's often challenging to know exactly when we become aware of new things, but I believe it happens with great regularity. And when we do realize that we are awakened to something new, we are both amazed by how significant this new knowing actually is, while at the same time perplexed by how it could possibly be that we've been so unaware for as long as we have.

That's the essence of the hurried life. That's the kind of distracted existence that the Adversary is hoping will side-track us long enough to keep the With-God life both out of sight and out of mind.

But the With-God life requires that we make every effort to become more aware of *how* we live and *why* we live the way(s) that we do. God wants us to choose what we fill our days with. God wants us to live with greater intention. But slowing, and Sabbath-keeping, is very foreign to how our world functions and how we have been trained to live. Learning to live at a different pace of life is not as easy as it might sound.

Going Slow at Going Slow

Just like the practice of silence, the practice of slowing and Sabbath-keeping is something we should not assume we can just make happen. Even the smallest of changes to how we live will naturally lead us to experience some tension in both our inner and outer worlds, where we can expect to face some level of pushback or resistance.

Adopting spiritual practices into our hurried lives, designed to bring measured and noticeable change to the pace at which we live, need to be both intentional and incremental. We need to go slow at going slow. We need to learn how to live at a pace other than overdrive.

And learning takes time.

If we really want change to happen, and for it to be long-lasting and fruit-bearing, we need to be willing to give it the time and space it needs in order to take root in our life.

What Might It Look Like to Begin to Practice Sabbath?

Learning to practice slowing and Sabbath-keeping can take on a wide variety of forms and expressions, but here are a few entry-level efforts that might serve you well in your early attempts to bring change to your hurried life.

Go to church. This one might seem both obvious, and a little out of place. But I choose to include it because I think that Sunday is the most likely candidate for a day (or partial day) of rest. Going to church is increasingly countercultural, and has a similar kind of reorienting affect that Sabbath is supposed to in our life.

I know far too many college students that make excuse upon excuse for why they can't find a local church to belong to, or don't make it out of bed in time to get to church on most weekends. They attempt to convince themselves that they listen to enough podcasts and worship music to make up for it, but it's not the same.

If a part of Sabbath is the reorientation of your gaze (not to mention your heart and priorities), going to church on a regular basis is a great way to help with this.

Set aside some time. Carve out some space in your schedule to do nothing. Consider it a calendar sacrifice to God. It may only be an hour or two in the beginning, but decide to do it and then follow through. It may feel odd or awkward in your early attempts, but the only way to learn to set aside time is to actually set aside time. Don't set an agenda or plan how you might mentally fill this void in your calendar. Instead, just plan to show up and know that at the very least you have chosen to honor God by clearing this space in your busy day.

Go for a walk. Walks are slow. Walks without a destination or agenda often give us the chance to become more aware of, and better in tune with, our surroundings.

Go someplace with an incredible view. Learning how to be still can be a real challenge. But identifying a beautiful place where you could be still for a while, with the task of simply sitting and observing, could be a great first step as you learn to practice slowing and stopping. As you arrive at your location, find someplace comfortable to sit (or walk), and allow yourself to soak in your surroundings. Pay close attention to the different details of your site—the sounds, the smells, the views. Give yourself plenty of time and remind yourself that there's no agenda for this time. You're simply there to take it all in—which ultimately is taking in the Creator God and his work all around you.

Get good sleep. I don't know many students that get good sleep—at least not consistently. Most students I know I would consider binge sleepers. They regularly starve themselves of sleep because their days are crammed full of class, activities, work, other opportunities, and, of course, a social life. This leaves the late-night hours to deal with the impending homework, papers, projects, and looming exams.

But getting decent sleep is essential to learning how to practice Sabbath. Sleep deprivation will cause you to live life with one eye sleepily on what's happening in front of you while the other is restlessly looking for an opportunity to take five minutes for a little snooze. When we're sleep deprived we're barely functional. It's like we're on autopilot, which means that our gaze is likely to be blurred at best—and definitely not looking for God's activity in our midst.

Different people need different amounts of sleep to function at their best. You need to figure out what this amount is for you and then begin to protect this time. If that means eliminating things from your hurried life to get the sleep you need then be willing to make this sacrifice.

Take a nap. As a college student (who was probably living my own kind of hurried existence), I can remember being told by one of my campus leaders that, "sometimes a nap is the most spiritual thing you can do today." They weren't suggesting that I was some sort of amoral lost cause, but instead that I might best please God (and help myself) by taking a break from my chaotic schedule for a midday siesta.

Choosing to take a nap, instead of any of the countless other things that you could be doing with your time, is choosing to prioritize rest. Now, not all rest is Sabbath rest, but it does have the potential to be. We have the opportunity to acknowledge God, and honor God, when we break from our schedules for the sake of slowing, stopping, and resting. Taking a nap can indeed be a spiritual activity.

Take on less. This is another countercultural calling—to take on less, not more. Now, taking on too much is not a problem that everyone has. In my book, *CAMPUS gODS: Exposing the Idols That Can Derail Your Present and Destroy Your Future*, I identify the gOD of Ir/Responsibility. It was the only two-headed god that I named, and described how many students struggle to identify a responsible load to carry and schedule to keep. Most students I know tend toward one of two ends of the responsibility spectrum—either that of overcommitment or under-involvement.

Without stereotyping and pigeonholing, more often than not it is guys who fall to the under-involvement end of the spectrum while the ladies will more often than not tend toward the overcommitted side of the spectrum. The problem is that both ends of this spectrum can prove to be equally harmful. The challenge is to find that sweet spot in the middle of the spectrum where, on top of your school work (that one thing that you are paying a lot of money to be about), you find one or two things that you can really commit yourself to and you say no to the rest.

Learning to say no is critical to bringing your calendar under control and living a more intentional (and less hurried) kind of life.

Pay close attention to your calendar. Take some time each week to plan out your week. Identify your busier times of the day and week and attempt to create some appropriate space for slowing, stopping, and resting.

If you're not one for keeping a calendar, a great exercise for you might be to record everything you do over the course of a few days or even a week. When do you wake? How do you spend your time? Who do you spend your time with? How much time do you give to specific tasks or meetings or experiences? What are the repeating items on your calendar? What do you spend most of your time doing? Do the priorities you profess to have play out in your schedule? What might you need to do to have your calendar better reflect your priorities?

Many believe that you can tell what others think is important by observing on what they spend their money. While I agree with this, I think we can tell just as much about a person's priorities by looking at how they spend their time. Money is a form of currency that we all have in differing amounts. Time, on the other hand, is a currency of which we all have the exact same amount. God wants us to be good stewards of the time we are given each day.

Pay attention to how you feel throughout the day. Equally important to what we are doing all day is how we are feeling. Hurry is not just physical, but can be mental and emotional as well. Are there things throughout our day that evoke elevated levels of emotions, or weigh on our minds more heavily? How prevalent are these taxing items on your calendar? How much time do they consume each week? How much more time do we spend dealing with the mental preparation ahead of time, and the emotional aftermath well beyond the actual experience?

Take some time to journal your feelings within your calendar system. Ask God to reveal to you things of which you might not be aware. Ask God to give you the courage to deal with anything that might need to be addressed and changed.

Participate, don't lead. Another great exercise for those of us prone to the hurried life is to opt to participate in things instead of leading them. Our need to produce and perform can tend to push us toward leadership in a wide variety of contexts. And who doesn't want be viewed as a leader? Once identified as a leader, leadership opportunities can begin to present themselves with increasing regularity. And out of a desire to help and lead, the temptation to become all things to all people will begin to weasel its way into your life.

Making the choice to participate, and allow others to lead, is a great way to practice Sabbath in the midst of the regular activities of your day.

How Might You Know If It's Working?

Remember, the spiritual disciplines are not about getting results. But when you consistently engage them, and faithfully pursue God through your intentional practice of them, God will regularly produce fruit in your life as a by-product.

Presence. One of the gifts of Sabbath is presence. Breaking from your daily rhythms and routines, your obsession with productivity and accomplishment, you will be able to give all of that time, energy, and effort to something else— or someone else.

It might be that this break allows space for God to break in to your controlled world such that you're reoriented to his ever-presence in your life—and challenged to make change. Or maybe it's that this gift of Sabbath allows you to be more present with those people who are around you. Those who are closest to you. Those people that may tend to receive your leftovers after a hard day or a week's worth of work. It is likely both.

Presence is a hard thing to manufacture on your own human effort, but it becomes a more natural way of being when you consistently practice Sabbath.

Focus. Sabbath has a way of helping us to better see the tree through the forest. To focus on the thing that is right in front of us. And to give one thing the appropriate attention that it deserves. Focus of mind and focus of heart are closely linked in this way. When you allow yourself the chance to regularly slow down and rest, your ability to see and understand what is most important—and then give it your undivided attention—grows.

Peace. This may be one of the most obvious benefits from consistently practicing Sabbath. Peace is the antithesis of the hurried life. Hurried people often look at peaceful people as if they're lazy or crazy. *There's so much to do! How can you possibly be so calm?* But Jesus' words should reassure you that the kind of peace that comes from breaking from the pace of the world around you will help you to better understand the significance of Sabbath:

> Therefore I tell you, do not worry about your life, what you will eat or drink; or about your body, what you will wear. Is not life more than food, and the body more than clothes? Look at the birds of the air; they do not sow or reap or store away in barns, and yet your heavenly Father feeds them. Are you not much more valuable than they? Can any one of you by worrying add a single hour to your life? (Matt. 6:25–27)

Worry and hurry are kissing cousins. Peace is the gift that calms the storms that these two like to stir up.

Play. Play is a gift that we are unaware of as children, because it's all we know, except for what we see in most of those who are older than us—which doesn't often reflect what a gift play truly is. As children we love to play, but long to grow up and earn more serious responsibilities, and all of the accolades that come with them. We learn, at a fairly young age, that play isn't something our North American culture values very much, so we set it aside and fill our schedules with more important kinds of activities.

But the college years are well-suited to help you recapture and re-envision this important gift of play as a way of practicing Sabbath. With so much of your time being flexible and shaped by your will and desires, making play a priority becomes a right (and even responsibility) that you have. The ways that you prioritize and incorporate play into your college years will dictate to a high degree how you will do so for years after you graduate.

Depth. Depth is another expression of Sabbath. Richard Foster wrote that, "The desperate need today is not for a great number of intelligent people, or gifted people, but for deep people."[1] He went on to say that, "The classical Disciplines of the spiritual life call us to move beyond surface living into the depths. They invite us to explore the inner caverns of the spiritual realm. They urge us to be the answer to a hollow world."[2] In a world that functions on superficiality as a life-blood, depth is a countercultural way of living and exposing others to the blessing of Jesus and Sabbath.

The fruit of Sabbath-keeping, and all spiritual disciplines, is not what they do in us, but in the ways they more deeply connect us to the heart of God. As our intimacy and union with God grows, it's impossible not to experience change and growth and transformation as a result.

Releasing the End Results

It's hard not to start with the end in mind. In fact, we've been taught from a very young age that the start of any project should be a visualization of what the finished product will look like. This way we know what we're working toward. The mental image of our finished product will be a source of motivation for those times of frustration or struggle. Our predetermined end is how we know if or when we veer off course. It helps us to see where we've misstepped and offers us insight on how to get back on course.

But it's different with the spiritual disciplines. In fact, we must regularly remind ourselves that when we enter into the practice of spiritual disciplines, our job is not to define a destination, but simply to commit to the journey. When we release control of our expectations regarding the desired outcome of our efforts, we get out of God's way, and we surrender ourselves to a process in which we only play a partial role. We concede that we are destined to play a particular role, in the present moment, and confess that we don't know much beyond that. Yet we choose to trust God and remain faithful to the process.

This is true of our efforts as they relate to Sabbath-keeping and overcoming our hurried pace of life.

CHAPTER SEVEN

Crowds

Our fear of being alone
drives us to noise and crowds.
—Richard Foster, *Celebration of Discipline*

When he saw the crowds, he had compassion on
them, because they were harassed and helpless,
like sheep without a shepherd.
—Matthew 9:36

I have five small children. Yes, it's true. In fact, many would probably say that I live with a crowd. As funny as that may be, one of the scarier experiences I have had as a parent to all of these little ones is getting separated from them in a crowded place. It's not that we're reckless in the ways we move about. Things like this just happen from time to time—and it evokes extreme emotions of fear, panic, and terror within me for those moments that I cannot put an eye on one of my precious little ones.

There are other times when we're out in public and while I am very aware of where my little tribe members are, one of them might suddenly get turned around, or grab on to the leg of someone other than mommy or daddy, and in that instant realize that they don't know where they are—or where mommy and daddy are—and an instant panic sets in and a meltdown quickly ensues.

Crowds, when we're younger, can be a very scary place.

But at some point along life's journey, crowds are recast and re-presented to us, not as something to fear, but as a place to fit in. A place to belong. Or even, if we want, a place to hide out or get lost. Crowds go from being a place filled with strangers and dangers to the place we want to be— because it's where *everyone* else is. We don't want to be seen as *different*. We don't want to be known as an *outsider*. So we do whatever we have to do in order to become a part of the crowd.

We opt in to the crowds of life.

Crowded Places

We live in a crowded world. There's no two ways about it. In fact, it's rare that we ever find ourselves in a place and think, *I wonder where everyone is.* And in those rare instances when this does happen, we are often washed over by waves of fear and anxiety that we've somehow missed the message about where we are supposed to be—because clearly it's not here.

In our culture we have come to identify crowds as a sign of *life*, a sign of *health*, a sign that the world is *as it should be*. When we enter an empty space we immediately question why it's empty. *What's wrong with this place?* we might wonder. We associate a lack of crowds with a place or space that is unpopular, unhealthy, or insignificant.

Our culture has trained us to look for the crowds—and to follow them.

And yet, how often do we find ourselves in crowded places and feel the frustration levels within us begin to surge? Rush hour, the malls during the holidays, the DMV, the TSA lines at the airport, the drive-thru lanes during the lunch hour, the bookstore lines at the beginning and end of each term, the movie theater on opening night, just about any restaurant we might want to eat at on a Friday or Saturday evening, and on and on I could go. The point I'm attempting to make is simple: we've learned to attach a high value to crowds, but there are still several instances when we absolutely detest crowds—and I don't know that we associate these two worlds in the ways we should.

A Brimming Campus

Most campuses have recognized this cultural affinity toward crowds and found ways to follow suit. From the images found in most admissions materials, to the ways they market the cafeteria and workout facility, to the ways they program the evenings and weekends on campus—most institutions have come to recognize that students want to be where things are happening, where things are fun, and where they can readily connect with one another. While smaller numbers might be touted within the classroom, it's the vibrancy of the campus life outside of the classroom that has the attention of most students (and their parents) when deciding where to attend.

From the moment you show any level of interest in a school, they begin to flood you with e-mails and mailers riddled with images of crowds—crowds of which *you* could become a part. Upon arriving on campus, the message of crowds is converted to community, but the implications remain the same—where the masses are is where you should be as well. Concerts, sporting events, the cafeteria, residence hall activities, etc. They're all pumped up and pointed to as the place to be.

Campuses often take this a step further by creating traditions that are intended to bring the generations of masses together. Homecoming is a great example of this kind of event. Students of past and present, along with their families, converge upon campus for the sake of being together and celebrating the collective experiences of the different generations that have shared the same campus space. In the crowds there is formed a collective identity that serves to brand you one way or another.

It's not that these events or experiences are bad or wrong. In fact, they do often point to signs of a healthy community as they create ample opportunities to be out, to be social, and to grow in relationship with others. The danger, however, comes when all we do is hop from crowd to crowd without ever taking time to be alone. With a campus calendar full of opportunities, it is entirely possible to surround yourself with others at almost all hours of the day. And even when you finally make your way back to a quiet dorm room, you're never really alone.

Connected in Every Way

That's right. Even when we're alone, we're not really alone. Our technologies now allow us to be a part of the crowd—even when we're sitting in the solitude of our quiet dorm room or apartment. Cell phones and smart phones allow us to make calls, send texts, and chat face-to-face with anyone, from anywhere, at any point in time—day or night. We have been given the technology to take our crowds with us wherever we go. We don't have to be alone. And we can actually choose who we want to be with—even when there are others around. We can actually multiply the crowds in our world by combining the real and the virtual.

Social media has also created the capacity for us to tap into near limitless crowds—where we can watch from the shoreline, slowly wade into the shallows, or plunge ourselves into the deep end of the social media abyss. The time lines and news feeds of these places run like a New York stock ticker—constantly updating with people's new posts and pictures.

But have you ever stopped to consider why you feel so tied to the crowd? Why you feel drawn to the masses? Have you ever stopped to figure out what's behind your need to be connected at virtually every waking minute of your day?

If not, you may be surprised.

A Fear of Being Alone

One of the primary reasons we are attracted to crowds is because we fear being alone. We fear what people might think of us if we're seen alone. But even more, we fear what we might encounter if we are alone for any length of time at all.

We fear the solitude. Most of us don't like the idea of being alone. Not even for a short period of time. Being alone produces within us feelings of being lonely. Instead of seeing solitude as a place to be recharged and refocused we more often struggle with feelings of anxiety over when it will end—so we can return to the crowds. We don't know what to do with ourselves in solitude. It feels unproductive and lonesome—and in many ways vulnerably exposed.

We fear the silence. In solitude we often encounter silence as well. The solitude and silence hit us like a one-two punch, striking sharp contrast to the crowds and noise that so often fill our days. Silence, on top of the challenge of solitude, can feel like a heavy, wet blanket to the person who struggles to know how to exist in a setting like this. Not having anyone to be with or talk to can make us feel trapped and terrified. In silence, we are left to ourselves, and whatever lies within. And for most of us, not knowing what exactly awaits us within, we choose the comfort and familiarity of crowds and noise.

We fear encountering our true self—and not liking it. When stripped of the crowds that we often surround ourselves with, we can tend to find a person that we know not. When others constantly surround us, it becomes all too easy to take on, at least in part, the collective identity of the masses. And we know that when we do this, when we look and sound like those around us, we are more likely to find acceptance. But when we remove the crowds, and their far-reaching influence, we rarely know what exactly we'll find. In fact, one of the reasons I believe we are attracted to the masses is because we don't like who we are apart from them.

We fear finding God. Most of us struggle to believe that we are fully loved and accepted by God—just as we are. We know that we're not perfect, and have done some things that we'd rather not have to think about, so the idea of being alone and possibly having to confront these things—or even worse, having God confront us with these things—can be petrifying. On one hand, we've always longed for a close, intimate relationship with the One True God. But on the other hand, knowing our own spiritual shortcomings, we've never wanted to get too close out of a fear of what we might learn—about ourselves and/or God.

We fear not finding God. The only thing potentially more horrifying than encountering God in our solitude is not finding him there. I think most of us are content to live with the hope, or belief, that in the stillness we will find God.

But if we're honest, I don't know that most of us want to put that to the test. What would happen if we actually entered into solitude in search of God and didn't find him there? What would that do to our faith?

Crowds definitely present themselves as the safer, more comfortable alternative to solitude and being alone.

A Hidden Identity

In crowds, we are sufficiently able to fit in and fly under the radar. We are able to wear masks and disguises and be whoever we want to be—or whoever we think others want us to be. Crowds often afford us the opportunity to be different things to different people simply because we can.

In crowds, we have more anonymity, which allows us not to have to make clear-cut decisions about what we believe and how we're going to live out those beliefs. In crowds, we simply follow the lead and example of the crowd, and our beliefs and decisions are made for us. In crowds, we can hide who we really are, from ourselves and from others. And sometimes living a facade is easier, or more exciting, than living the life that God has given us to live.

Group Think

Crowds allow us freedom from having to think for ourselves —and risk thinking something that goes against the cultural grain. When we're a part of the masses it becomes easier to simply put our finger to the wind and understand what direction popular thought appears to be moving—and then to go in that direction. In many respects, crowds allow us to function on autopilot. We know that we're charting the right course simply by looking around and making sure that we're still with the crowd. This allows us freedom from having to struggle through issues that we are faced with every day.

A Different Kind of World

What we may or may not realize is that this crowded world in which we live and move and have our being is not conducive to the spiritual life. Dutch-born Catholic priest, professor, and author Henri Nouwen wrote, "Our society is not a community radiant with the love of Christ, but a dangerous network of domination and manipulation in which we can easily get entangled and lose our soul."[1] The way of the crowd is rarely the way of Christ. It's not that the crowd is always doing things that are inherently wrong or blatantly disruptive to the With-God life, but our Adversary has a way of utilizing the crowd, and our fixation upon it, to misguide us just enough to where we likely aren't aware of what we're doing or where we're going.

God wants this life to count. We should want this life to count as well. But that means that we cannot operate on autopilot. We cannot allow crowds to be our moral compass. We cannot allow the current direction of the masses to be what defines our priorities in life. The crowds cannot be this for us—because they rarely ever reflect the heartbeat of God. And even in those rare instances when they do, God still wants us to look to him, over and above any crowd.

What Are We Missing?

Do we see, understand, or even care what's happening here? The crowds that we incessantly surround ourselves with are distracting us from the With-God life.

Nouwen went on to write:

Our calendars are filled with appointments, our days and weeks filled with engagements, and our years filled with plans and projects. There is seldom a period in which we do not know what to do, and we move through life in such a distracted way that we do not even take the time and rest to wonder if any of the things we think, say, or do are worth thinking, saying, or doing.[2]

We have become the sheep without a shepherd that Jesus laments over when he observes the crowds and huddled masses.

This isn't the kind of With-God life that God desires for us. And I can assure you that you will not experience this kind of life by following the crowds. In fact, in order to find God, in order to experience him in ways that you've likely never experienced him before, you will need to be willing to leave the masses behind and intentionally seek out solitude.

CHAPTER EIGHT

Solitude

Anyone who wants to fight his demons
with his own weapons is a fool.
—Henri J. M. Nouwen, *The Way of the Heart*

We are relational beings. We have been created by a relational God to be in relationship with him and with others. A review of the Ten Commandments or Old Testament reveals law upon law designed to bring shape to our relationship with God and with others. Even Jesus, and the vast majority of public teachings that made up his three years of ministry, focused on how we relate to God and others. We are designed for relationship—to need God and others.

So the call to solitude—a voluntary withdrawal from community and the presence of others—may very well be the most unnatural practice we might pursue. It seems to go against the grain of our being on so many different levels. And clearly we live in a society that does not see the importance of solitude or the need to create space for it. And yet, this is exactly where God invites us to meet with him.

The With-God life is not one that will be found amidst the masses or noisy crowds of our everyday way of life. Does God exist in those places? Of course. But most of us are unable to recognize the presence of God when we're surrounded by so many people and distractions. Gary Holloway wrote, "In a life surrounded by distractions and noise, we must find ourselves and find God in solitude."[1]

The Desert, the Forest

One of the reasons that we so often struggle with the thought of solitude is because the very idea of choosing to be alone is so foreign to our crowded existence. Even if we wanted to get away from it all (which we're not too sure that we would ever want to anyway), how would we go about accomplishing such a task?

In talking about the practice of solitude, it's not uncommon to hear people refer to more remote, isolated locations, like a forest or desert. These places can be both literal and metaphorical, but are meant to describe the kind of environment where we might more easily encounter and commune with the One True God.

Now, depending on the kind of person you are, you will likely look at these kinds of places in one of two ways: 1) a more peaceful place filled with beauty, mystery, wonder, and potential, or 2) a more lonely, scary, potentially dangerous environment where harmful and evil things await. And I suppose that in reality, both of these views can hold some level of truth, especially as it relates to solitude.

Solitude is an invitation into a lonely, potentially scary and dangerous place—where we may indeed encounter harmful or evil things within us. But we do this because we believe that this is where we might more readily encounter God and be awakened to the kinds of peace, beauty, mystery, wonder, and potential that the With-God life is intended to be filled—and that may not be uncovered in any other way.

Richard Foster noted that, "Solitude is more a state of mind and heart than it is a place. There is a solitude of the heart that can be maintained at all times."[2] But in order for many of us to get to this state of mind and heart, some trips to a more literal desert or forest or place of solitude will likely be required.

A Deep, Inner Detachment

The point of solitude is not simply the separation of self from others. According to Dallas Willard:

> In solitude, we purposefully abstain from interaction with other human beings, denying ourselves companion-ship and all that comes from our conscious interaction with others. . . . The normal course of day-to-day human interactions locks us into patterns of feeling, thought, and action that are geared to a world set against God. Nothing but solitude can allow the development of a freedom from the ingrained behaviors that hinder our integration into God's order.[3]

In the desert, we allow ourselves to be stripped away from the pieces of this world that seek to shape us and form us into an image other than God's. In the desert, we allow God to shine a bright light into the recesses of our life in ways that bring clarity, healing, and a necessary reordering of life.

As important as it is for us to regularly choose to practice solitude, it is not easy, nor does it quickly produce the kind of fruit that we might hope something so radical should do. In the desert, we are made painfully aware of the things of this world that we hold dear, that we deem important, and that we allow to define our own meaning and sense of self. In the forest, we are challenged to distance, and even detach, ourselves from those things that are not in alignment with the will and desires of God. Solitude becomes an opportunity we are given, every time we enter into it, to see the things of this world with the eyes of Jesus and then to choose the will and ways of God for our life.

Encountering the One True God

There is nothing more powerful than an encounter with the One True God. The practice of the discipline of solitude is what creates the atmosphere for this kind of encounter. Remember, he wants us to want him more than we want anything else. And even though we are designed as relational beings, sometimes we are called to temporarily withdraw from all other relationships so that our sole attention might be focused on God alone. And this, after all, should be the desire of our hearts as followers of Jesus. Right?

We've likely prayed a prayer and confessed some beliefs at some point in our life, and attempted to live the kind of life that we think would honor God—at least most of the time. But if you're anything like me, then you probably wonder from time to time if all of this belief and sacrifice and effort is amounting to much more than an overspiritualized list of convictions, practices, and striving.

We confess our love for God, and believe that he loves us back, or that he's loved us long before we ever loved him. But we wonder if there's supposed to be more to it. We hope that there's more in store for us *this* side of heaven.

We wonder if we could ever have the kind of burning-bush encounter that Moses had in the Bible. We wonder if we could have the kind of intimacy with God that we see in King David. We wonder if we would ever be viewed by God in the ways that he viewed the prophets before Jesus, and therefore deemed worthy to live and model a life that is contrary to everyone around us. We wonder, if Jesus were to come back today, if he'd choose us to be a part of his ragtag crew and the beginning of his church.

Solitude is the place for such encounters and messages to be experienced. Again, it's not that God cannot, or will not, speak to us in other, more crowded, places or spaces. But our reality is that we've belonged to a culture that has long learned to crowd God out. So if we have any hope of experiencing God in deep and profound ways in this lifetime, then we'd better avail ourselves to the regular practice of solitude.

The Refiner's Fire

Our times in solitude are not just about encountering God, or creating a less-crowded space in which God might better have our attention, but so that the One True God might more easily have his way in our life. Henri Nouwen wrote that, "Solitude is the furnace of transformation."[4] If we want to be changed and transformed by God, more and more into the likeness of Christ, then we will choose to engage in the practice of solitude.

"It is in this solitude that we discover that being is more important than having, and that we are worth more than the result of our efforts. In solitude we discover that our life is not a possession to be defended, but a gift to be shared."[5] The choice of solitude puts our lives in the crucible and allows God to burn away all of the impurities. It's a stripping down of all of the false identities and overexaggerated accomplishments that we so readily hide behind, such that we are before God with nothing to offer, but there only to be loved and accepted as we are.

This is where God wants us. And this is where God can best work within us and more readily use us in the lives of others. When we allow God the opportunity to reduce us to what he originally created us to be, separate and distinct from what the crowds of our world tell us we should do or be, then we're ready to be shaped and molded into something that is truly useable in the hands of God.

Again, it's important to be aware of the fact that the refiner's fire is not a pleasant or easy thing to experience. The stripping away, the burning off of impurities, they all serve to reveal to us those things that we have held most intensely—and even in the presence of the One True God they can be very hard to let go of. But as we are faithful to God, and continue to place ourselves before him as we practice solitude, we find that God is faithful and just and willing to do new and amazing things within us.

Face-to-Face With the True You

Although I briefly mentioned it in the previous section, it's important that we circle back to explore this idea of true self and false self. While we might believe ourselves to be fairly authentic and genuine followers of Jesus, we will likely be surprised by what is revealed to us in our practice of solitude.

We have long lived in a culture of comparison and achievement. Although we want to belong to the crowd, we still have desires to be seen as separate and distinct in our own right. We want to be known as great, or special, or even as the best. When this doesn't happen naturally, we find ways to compensate—or overcompensate. There may be some things that we've knowingly done or said to make ourselves look or sound a certain way. There are likely many more things that we've unknowingly done or said for the exact same reasons. For most of our lives we've been creating an image, a persona, or maybe several of them. And this is one of the reasons we seek out crowds.

But solitude is no place for facades or false identities. God knows us already, so the only person that we might be attempting to dupe in solitude is ourselves. As we enter into these times, God's penetrating light and love wear down and wipe away the false identities that we have learned to hide behind, leaving only our true selves. These true selves are something that may seem quite foreign in nature, although strangely familiar. These true selves might be something we've knowingly been trying to run from, or even deny, but it is the only self that God wants us to know and live out of.

God has made us all unique in our own right. And although our culture has chosen certain traits and attributes to fixate on—and uphold as the ideal—God did not make a mistake when he made you or me. He made us exactly as he desired for us to be—and finding your true self is a part of reclaiming your original identity as a beloved daughter or son of God.

Solitude helps to facilitate this process.

Seeing the Tree Through the Forest

Solitude is one of the biggest risk/reward disciplines that I've dared to practice during my life as a follower of Jesus. Each of the spiritual disciplines has its own set of challenges and potential fruit. But for me, solitude feels more risky than some of the others. It's not about me or what I can do, but about learning who I am and how I can relate to God when everything is stripped away. It's incredibly vulnerable. But I think it holds the potential to yield some of the greatest transformation.

When we engage in the regular practice of solitude, and allow God to search us and change us, we are conformed more and more into the image of Jesus. We see growth and greater intimacy in our relationship with God and with others. And when these things are given over to God, he has a way of bringing alignment and clarity to the other areas of our life.

Gary Thomas captured the essence of potential that's found in practicing solitude when he wrote, "All I know is that it's in those solitary moments that colors regain their brightness, truth regains its clarity, and reality loses its fog. Without some time alone, I feel like I've lost my anchor."[6] Solitude allows us to see the forest for what it really is and to be able to focus on the specific tree that God places before us.

Alone for the Sake of Others

German Lutheran pastor, theologian, and anti-Nazi dissident Dietrich Bonhoeffer once said, "Let him who cannot be alone beware of community. He will only do harm to himself and to the community."[7] The work that happens in solitude has ramifications for our life in community.

Our practice of solitude, and ongoing growth and transformation as a child of God, is not just for our own benefit, but for the benefit of others as well. I believe this is what God has always intended for us—as holy and set-apart ones—we've just lost this understanding in our crowded, me-centered existence. We see this so clearly in God's first covenant, established with Abraham, when he stated: "I will make you into a great nation, and I will bless you; I will make your name great, and you will be a blessing. I will bless those who bless you and whoever curses you I will curse; *and all peoples on earth will be blessed through you*" (Gen. 12:2–3, emphasis added).

Blessed to be a blessing.

God wants to shape us and grow us, through the discipline of solitude, and all the others, so that we might be more faithful in our relationship with him and others, and so that we might be a blessing to others through how we live our lives.

So what, exactly, might it look like to begin to practice the discipline of solitude?

CHAPTER NINE

Learning to Be Alone— and with Others

E ven after reading a chapter on all of the potential benefits that can be gleaned from engaging in the regular
practice of solitude, I'd be willing to bet that you're still not
so sure about this particular discipline. Unless you're an
extreme introvert, the idea of seeking out solitude just seems
so counter to everything that is within us. We cherish people
and want to be around them. We don't choose to be alone.
We don't willfully withdraw from others.

But that's why it's called a discipline, right?

They don't come naturally, so we have to practice them.
We have to train ourselves by starting small and taking on
more manageable experiences. The apostle Paul talks of

beating his body and making it a slave to him (instead of being a slave to it). He also talks about going into training and running with the intent of winning the race (see 1 Corinthians 9:24–27). Paul was a smart guy, and knew that in order to experience the With-God life, followers of Jesus would have to learn to live disciplined lives. They would have to prioritize practices that would put them in position to be molded and shaped by God because normal day-to-day life would not naturally facilitate this kind of thing.

The words of the author of the book of Hebrews have been seared in my memory since my own college experience: "No discipline seems pleasant at the time, but painful. Later on, however, it produces a harvest of righteousness and peace for those who have been trained by it" (Heb. 12:11). Discipline is not something most of us are naturally attracted to. We don't like to withhold things from ourselves because it doesn't feel good and it goes against the messages of our culture. Instant gratification has become the cultural norm by which we now compare everything else. We don't believe we should withhold anything from ourselves. Messages from our mainstream media and North American culture only serve to reinforce these internal impulses. But this kind of mentality, that lacks discipline in every way, is really a ruse. It feels good in the moment, but produces a whole lot of nothing in the long run. It is the discipline and the commitment we make to be consistent and persistent in our pursuit of Jesus that God uses to produce a bounty of righteousness, peace, and the like within us.

We Enter In Slowly

True of all of the disciplines, but maybe even more so with solitude, we must be willing to take things slow. We must be willing to be a beginner and approach our practice of solitude as a true beginner would and should.

We must choose more elementary ways of engaging solitude, knowing that God can meet us in those places just as easily as he can through some of the more advanced practices. What God really cares about is our heart and mind. He wants these things focused on him and available to the ways in which he'd like to work upon them.

Solitude, with its limitless depths and relentless way of peeling back the revealing layers of our life, is probably best situated to scare us off from ever practicing it again—if we're not careful and measured in our early attempts at practicing this discipline. We must be willing to trust that God can do the work that he wants to do within us in our more basic practices, while also trusting that when it's time to wade into deeper waters that he'll let us know—and we'll actually be in a place where we can recognize his leading, and so follow.

We must take on the mindset of the tortoise. Slow and steady wins the race. We must learn to go slow and be okay with the results as they come. We cannot get into the comparison game with those around us—for their journey is theirs. It's not yours and it's not mine. And we cannot speed things up, or attempt to manufacture results in our life because we are unwilling to wait on God and wade into the waters of solitude. God has us on our own course and our job is to be faithful to that course. We choose a slow and steady pace because we don't want to burnout and fail to finish.

So we go slow. We practice solitude in small ways at first because we're beginners.

Little Solitudes Every Day

Richard Foster suggested that a great way to begin to practice solitude is to look for the little solitudes that present themselves every day. This will obviously require that we become more aware of the rhythms and routines that make up our everyday living. Where are there some natural gaps? When do you seem to have some time and space that might allow you to withdraw—even if only for ten or fifteen minutes? Will your schedule lead you out near someplace that you might enjoy spending some quiet moments sitting or walking? A park or lake? A wooded trail?

Is there something you could incorporate into your preexisting schedule that would not feel like a great effort or burden? Maybe a time when your roommates are typically gone and your room is quieter. Possibly a morning or afternoon when you are free of class work and other responsibilities.

Yes, this will all feel like work in the beginning. Even hard work. But at some point, you will need to get over the hump of doing difficult things and resign yourself to doing it simply because it's what God desires of you.

Discomfort and our natural tendencies toward the path of least resistance will cause us to question our practice of solitude soon enough, so it will be important to experience some small wins through some easy, early engagements with solitude.

Find a Quiet Place

As we've previously explored, solitude is more of a head-and-heart reality than it is a physical location. But it can also be a physical location. In fact, I would suggest that before most of us can get to that head-and-heart reality, we're probably going to have to start out by engaging in the practice of solitude through actually going off and finding a quiet place. Before we can deal with the noise and crowds of our inner world, we'll need to learn how to manage the noisy crowds of our outer world.

Finding a quiet place, while simple in theory, can prove to be a bit of a challenge. If you live on campus it may very well require that you get up early—yes, I said early. I recognize that most students like to sleep in as long as they can, but that's why early makes sense. With many of your friends and classmates still asleep, finding a quiet space in your apartment or somewhere on campus will be much more likely. Again, discipline is being willing to put yourself in unnatural, uncomfortable positions so that you might be more readily available to God. Sacrificing a little sleep should seem inconsequential compared to the prospect of growing deeper in relationship with God.

Going off campus is always an option as well. The challenge, especially on busier days, is protecting the kind of time that it might require to actually get off campus to your designated quiet spot. So becoming a good manager of your time and schedule will be important, as will finding a good spot on campus that can be your go-to space when getting off campus just isn't an option. But knowing where you might go off campus, as time allows, is another great way to begin to practice solitude.

Go for a Walk, or Run, or Bike Ride

Taking some time to break from your normal rhythms and crowds, and opting to go outside for a little exercise in God's creation, is another great way to enter into the practice of solitude. Unless you choose a location that is packed with other walkers, runners, or bikers, you'll likely find yourself in less-crowded spaces, and better positioned to be reoriented to your surroundings in such a way that God seems to have more space to get your attention.

You'll be challenged to free up your mind and heart as you break away from the crowds. Don't be surprised if you find yourself wondering, and even worrying, about what you might be missing back on campus. Remind yourself you'll be okay. As you pursue uncrowded spaces, be willing to give God the things that weigh on your heart and mind, so that your early efforts in solitude don't take on an unhealthy or unhelpful design.

Let Your Words Be Few

One of the ways that you can begin to cultivate an inner solitude—a heart and mind that are able to get quiet and close out the distractions around you—is to simply choose to talk less. Identify a specific day and time that will fit within the makeup of your schedule and decide that during this period you will do your best to limit your words. You might choose a time when you know your interaction with others will be minimal, but you might also practice this kind of effort in the presence of others. You don't want to do anything that will hurt or hinder any of your relationships, so you will need to respond to the questions of those you are with, but your goal will be to keep from speaking excessively or with an agenda.

It's amazing how a choice to hold one's tongue can bring peace and clarity to one's heart and mind. When we're not trying to come up with a witty one-liner, or a clever retort, or even a thoughtful insight to share, God can find the space within us to begin to do a new work.

Small Acts of Service

Doing small acts of service, preferably in secret, is another great way of entering into the practice of solitude. I realize this may seem contradictory to what I've previously stated with regard to solitude being about *being* and not *doing*. But if you are a doer, jumping right into *not doing* is going to be a stretch.

One of the ways that you can break from the patterns and priorities of our culture, and begin to take steps toward solitude, is by finding smaller, less obvious ways of assisting others. It could be something like straightening up your room without your roommate having to ask. It could be picking up after someone in the cafeteria. It could entail helping someone get their groceries from the parking lot to their room. It could involve folding someone else's laundry while you wait for your load to finish.

I think you get the idea. What these little acts of service do is ever so subtlety take the focus off of self and place it on another. It may only be for a few moments, but it serves to break into a natural obsession with self, and creates a more likely space for God to get your attention—and eventually your focus.

Retreat and Let Your Life Speak

In a lot of ways, a retreat is like a mini-vacation, but you're *not doing* instead of *doing*. And in your not doing, you take the time and space and offer it to God. You're choosing to be present in God's presence. Depending on how long you retreat, and how long you've been participating in retreats, you may also begin to incorporate other spiritual disciplines like prayer, meditation, and fasting into this time.

Retreating could probably be considered more of an intermediate practice, but shorter (half-day) retreats can be taken on by beginners in their early practice of solitude if they are feeling somewhat comfortable with this particular discipline.

The key to retreats, no matter how long their duration, is to make sure that you allow for plenty of unprogrammed, unstructured time. Go in without an agenda other than giving God your time and focused attention and hoping that he might choose to speak into your life. Solitude is a place for you to encounter God and encounter your true self. And when you create space for God to speak, or for God to reveal or illuminate some of the areas in your life that might need attention, you want to be in a receiving posture. You want to be ready to hear what's being said, or see what's being revealed, without distractions of your own making.

We Emerge Different—and Ready to Be with Others

It's important to remember that your times of solitude aren't just about breaking from the influences and priorities of the crowd. And they're not even solely about creating space for God to work more easily in your life—although this is important. Your times in solitude also have implications for the communities and crowds in which you are a part. Your practice of solitude is not just about cultivating a personal holiness, but about being shaped and formed for the sake of others. Your time alone informs the way(s) you understand and function within the context of community.

Solitude calls us from the presence of others into the presence of the One True God so that when we return to others we are closer to our best possible selves. When we allow God the opportunity to work on us, in the workshop of solitude, we come out changed as a result. And it's not that we now have something better to offer others in terms of what we can do, but much more to do with our ability to *be* better—both with God and with others.

Solitude calls us from the crowds of life, into the presence of the Holy, such that whether we are alone or with others we are more in tune with the activity of God in our midst—and we live differently as a result.

CHAPTER TEN

"Muchness" and "Manyness"

For where your treasure is,
there your heart will be also.
—Matthew 6:21

Simplicity is freedom. Duplicity is bondage.
Simplicity brings joy and balance.
Duplicity brings anxiety and fear.
—Richard Foster, *Celebration of Discipline*

I don't believe that we're born with a hunger for power and a need for control. But not long after we enter this world we become aware, even as infants, of hierarchies within life. Infants quickly pick up on the fact that if they want to be fed, or burped, or changed, or rocked to sleep that they will likely need to do a little fussing and whining—if not all-out wailing—in order to get the necessary attention and results that they're looking for.

As we get older we become increasingly aware of a struggle taking place, in a variety of ways and on an array of levels, all around us. We jockey for social position within our circles of friends (even as toddlers and early adolescents). We are awakened to what's cool and what's not, and feel compelled to do whatever we have to in order to keep up or redefine what cool is so that we're up toward the top of the social pyramid. We experience small tastes of success and defeat in a culture that is fixated on the pursuit of muchness and manyness. And before we know it, we are swept up in the cultural current of this malformed pursuit.

James, the brother of Jesus, wrote, "What causes fights and quarrels among you? Don't they come from your desires that battle within you? You desire but do not have, so you kill. You covet but you cannot get what you want, so you quarrel and fight. You do not have because you do not ask God" (James 4:1–2). James understood that our preoccupation with the treasures of this world, in all their different forms and fashions, would lead us *away* from God and *against* one another. Our pursuit of, obsession with, and addictions to the muchness and manyness of this world can take on many different forms and deceptively lead us far off from the path and pursuit of God.

Let's take a look at some of those deceptive forms now.

It's Material

When we talk about being caught up in muchness and manyness, we're definitely talking about a material level; this is the most obvious form of this unhealthy fixation. We may couch it in terms of living the American Dream, but the truth of the matter is that we are a consumeristic society that is all about meeting our every need, not denying ourselves anything, and continually looking for what's new and what's next.

We've been duped by an American machine that wants to sell us, well, everything, as well as an Enemy who wants to keep us distracted from the With-God life and fixated on the priorities of the world. We've become convinced that what will fill the voids in our life can all be found in the latest fashions, newest gadgets, and upsized possessions. We've been tricked into believing that if we can attain X, then we'll be happy, content, and able to move on with other things in life. But that is the classic lie of materialism that we are fed by our consumer culture and Adversary. They both want us to believe that our contentment is just around the corner, and when we get there, then we'll be satisfied.

So we feed our desires. We don't withhold anything from ourselves. We spend our money, and then we spend money we don't have, in order to get things that we don't need, ultimately finding ourselves feeling just as empty and unfulfilled.

On top of that, we run the dangerous risk of putting our financial future, as well as our overall happiness and ability to follow the leading of God in our life, at risk as we bury ourselves under a growing mass of debt, all for the sake of trying to keep pace with everyone around us. We see what they have, and we think we need it too, so whether we can afford it or not we go get it. We neglect any future implications because all we're focused on is the here and the now and how this new possession will bring us inconceivable amounts of joy, pleasure, and contentment.

What a sham.

It's Social

Our pursuit of muchness and manyness has a social element as well. In fact, for some of us, the social element may be a more dominant vice than the material. We are a culture that is obsessed with power, control, fame, and influence. We want to be known and valued and respected.

At a young age we learn to start angling for voice and social clout. We look for ways to assert leadership and dominance. We begin to believe, and attempt to convince others, that we know what's right, what's best, or what's going on to gain the most attention—and then insert ourselves at the front of the idea, movement, or work.

We are products of a culture that has long touted structures like power, control, fame, and influence as significant measures of success and happiness. We have become convinced that if we are able to make it to the top of the proverbial food chain, only then will we be positioned to do as we please or enact what we think will make a difference in the world.

Our Adversary can cast this desire in ways that are less self-seeking and aggrandizing, and much more noble and justice-minded. But when we begin to pursue anything above God, we allow it to become something that has power and control over us.

Much of this kind of social climbing is tied to what we believe about reputations and their role in our lives and the world in which we live. We see the way others are esteemed and we want what they have. But what we don't often know is what it took them to attain that kind of reputation and social standing. We don't know what they've endured or travailed. Most people of high standing and strong reputation have had to experience some pretty difficult things in life, and they've not only survived their struggles, but found ways to thrive in the midst of their adversity. They proved themselves to be people of honesty, integrity, and character and it earned them voice, respect, and social standing.

But we often want the latter without having to endure the former. We want the social power, control, fame, and influence but don't want to do anything to actually earn it.

It's Emotional

Our obsession with muchness and manyness has an emotional element. We are a culture that is obsessed with feeling good. We want safety, security, and every opportunity for happiness—no matter the cost. Much of our world is made up of people with underdeveloped or out-of-control egos that are in constant need of affirmation and stroking. Many of us lack resiliency and the ability to endure hardships or stand firm in the face of opposition. In many ways, our pursuit of muchness and manyness becomes a way to pacify our neediness within.

We buy new things because of how it makes us feel in the moment, or the first time we're seen in it or with it, and are typically surprised by how quickly the newness of it wears off.

We pursue positions of greater status because we believe that these new accomplishments or acquisitions are a mirrored reflection of how people will think about us. The more we attain, the greater people's view of us must be, and therefore the greater we will feel about ourselves. Yet, we tend to struggle when we bump up against the slightest pushback on how we use those same positions and status.

When we attach our sense of self and self-worth to the pursuit of muchness and manyness, our world becomes an unstable roller coaster of emotions that leaves us with greater levels of anxiety and frustration than it does peace, trust, and confidence.

It's Controlling

When we avail ourselves to the pursuit of muchness and manyness, we are really attempting to set the deck of life in our favor and bring the world under our control. Our need to control, our all-out obsession with control, speaks to our deep lack of faith in God and trust in his plan and place for our lives. Whether we're attempting to control people's perception of us, different relational dynamics, or desired outcomes for things, our attempts to control put us in an unhealthy, god-like position.

But what we don't realize is that in our attempts to control our environment, relationships, and reputation, we are actually being controlled and manipulated ourselves. It's true. Our Adversary is confusing us and distracting us by convincing us that we can actually control the lives we lead, as well as the lives and circumstances of those around us. If we can work hard enough, and maneuver a few things to go our way, and manipulate a few people to follow our lead, we believe that we will be on the path to greatness.

Yes, we do have some control over our own lives. And yes, we are meant to have a positive influence on the lives of others around us. But the moment we become convinced that we can control everything, we slip from reality to a dangerous and/or irrelevant place. Much like mice in a maze or hamsters on a wheel, we race about, believing that we are going somewhere, but we never really get anywhere; and we don't realize it until we are in an unhealthy and far-off place.

It's Self-Centered and Self-Indulgent

Our pursuit of muchness and manyness is really all about us. There's just no two ways about it. When we place the pursuit of muchness and manyness before us as a priority, we are communicating to everyone around us that we think we are the most important thing in the world. That we are the center of our universe. That our needs, wants, and desires are more important than anyone else's—including God's. I know this might sound a bit harsh or over the top, but it's true.

We would likely never conceive of it in these terms, especially when thinking about ourselves, but when our gaze is fixed on making much of *ourselves*—through our possessions, our reputation, our title, or our ability to influence—then there's no way that we could possibly be positioned to consider anyone or anything else. When our focus is on the things of this world, and what they might be able to afford us, we are unable to see the world as God does, and come into direct tension with the With-God life.

This line of thinking, and living, has a way of multiplying our own sense of self-importance. We buy into our own press and struggle when we don't see others doing the same. We think we're awesome and believe that everyone else should see us this way as well. If they don't, then we tend to believe that there's something wrong with them, *not us.*

It's Self-Reliant

Our fixation on muchness and manyness reveals a lack of trust in God. We don't believe he knows our needs, has the ability to adequately provide for us, or to socially position us where we most naturally will flourish. We think we know better than God.

When we take on this pursuit, we essentially push God aside with the belief that if he could just see things as we see them, and give us the desires of our heart (no matter how selfish or self-centered they are), that everything would be for the best. Without consideration for the timing of God, the purposes of God, or even the will of God, we're tempted to strike out to make things happen on our terms and in our strength.

We might even deceive ourselves into believing that God needs us to take this on, and use our own efforts, if we're going to accomplish what needs to be accomplished. We may even attempt to justify our pursuit of muchness and manyness by insisting that once we have the money, or the power, or the influence, that we'll then be able to serve God more faithfully.

But the reality is that this pursuit of muchness and manyness is a winding rabbit hole that will leave us lost and struggling to believe that we could ever find our way back to the path of God. And because we've been convinced that we can do things on our own, we put our heads back down and attempt to find our way out, instead of asking for God's grace and assistance.

It's a Chasing After the Wind

The author of the book of Ecclesiastes is believed to be King Solomon, even though he was never mentioned by name. King Solomon was said to have been the wisest person to have walked the earth (other than Jesus, we can assume), because when he was anointed king over Israel as a young boy, he asked God for wisdom to lead God's chosen people—over and above the power, wealth, fame, and influence of muchness and manyness. God was so pleased with Solomon's request that he blessed him with great wisdom and so much more.

The book of Ecclesiastes records Solomon's own pursuit of muchness and manyness. He pursued everything—wisdom, pleasure, fame, and fortune—and he found it all to be hollow and meaningless. A "chasing after the wind" is how he repeatedly described it all. He had access to absolutely everything that could have possibly been pursued as a means to produce happiness, contentment, and fulfillment in life. But it all amounted to nothing. The book of Ecclesiastes is really a jarring book to the casual reader, because it takes such a cynical look at life, and deems it all meaningless—a "chasing after the wind." Yet, in the final verses of this book, there is a point of clarity that concludes that the only thing that brings meaning and proper perspective to the rest of life is a right relationship with God.

There it is. The secret to life revealed. It's been there—in the Bible—all along. And yet somehow we've missed it and continue to miss it today.

These words of Richard Foster should serve for us as a warning flare shot high into the night sky: "It is time we awaken to the fact that conformity to a sick society is to be sick. Until we see how unbalanced our culture has become at this point, we will not be able to deal with the mammon spirit within ourselves nor will we desire Christian simplicity."[1]

And the spiritual practice of simplicity is exactly what we will need to engage in if we wish to deal with our own struggles with muchness and manyness, which is where we now turn.

CHAPTER ELEVEN

Simplicity

Watch out! Be on your guard against all
kinds of greed; life does not consist in
an abundance of possessions.
—Jesus, in Luke 12:15

Simplicity sets us free to receive the provision of
God as a gift that is not ours to keep and can be
freely shared with others.
—Richard Foster, *Celebration of Discipline*

When we're young, life is pretty simple. There's sleeping, eating, playing, eating, crying, and more sleeping. I don't remember what it was like to be a three-year-old, but I've currently got one. In fact, he's the fourth three-year-old that I've helped raise. I know the experts like to claim that it's the twos that are so terrible, but I tend to believe it's the three-year-olds that have it the toughest.

At the age of three, our little ones seem to be teetering on the edge of a new frontier. They have mostly mastered the skills of walking and talking and seem to be awakening to what the bigger kids around them are up to. They begin to think of themselves as a big kid and start to believe that they should, therefore, be allowed to do big-kid things. But that's never how we parents see it.

They're almost there, but not quite. There are new things that they'd like to try, and we'd like to let them try, but it would probably be irresponsible for us to do so at this point in time. So we don't let them. And they don't like that at all.

They've lived the simple life for as much of their life as they can remember, and have long watched and waited to be able to do what they see their older siblings, cousins, neighbors, and strangers doing. Riding the school bus, playing on sport teams, using electronics, and swimming in the deep end of the pool are just a few of the new things they'd like to try out for themselves. And as they grow, their dreams expand with regard for what their life might include. Always looking at those who are older, able to do more and take on more responsibility, for their cues.

They pine for a season when they will be older and freer to do as they please. But what they don't often recognize is that what they pine for, at least in part, is a more complex existence that is filled with pressures to keep up, and outperform, in a culture of muchness and manyness. And maybe those of us who are older have done too good of a job masking the complexities of our world from the younger generations. Or maybe we don't mask it at all, because we've fully bought into it. So instead of trying to hide this reality from our young ones we uphold this deadened pursuit as the ideal life.

The reality is that God does not desire our lives to be as complex as they are. He does not want us to get caught up in the rat race of muchness and manyness. He desires that we live lives that are holy and pleasing to him. But that kind of existence goes against much of the grain of our North American culture. In fact, it's so counter to the culture that we have few (if any) good models of what it means to live simply in our twenty-first century North American world.

But God gives us a way of fighting this fight.

Throughout history, God has faithfully met his children who have chosen a way of life that is simpler and counter to the culture. He offers us the same opportunity through the regular practice of the discipline of simplicity. Richard Foster wrote, "The central point for the Discipline of simplicity is to seek the kingdom of God and the righteousness of his kingdom first and then everything necessary will come in its proper order."[1] Put God first. Put his kingdom and priorities first. And from there, everything else in life will fall into its proper place. Simplicity gives us a single focus—a unity of heart and mind and spirit—as we make the conscious decision and effort to push aside the agendas of our world and fix our gaze solely on God and his priorities.

Foster captured the spirit of this discipline when he explained that, "Simplicity is freedom, not slavery. Refuse to be a slave to anything but God."[2] So let us now begin to explore this discipline of simplicity.

Seek First God's Kingdom

"Seeking first God's kingdom and the righteousness, both personal and social, of that kingdom is the only thing that can be central in the Spiritual Discipline of simplicity."[3] Clearly Foster was building a case for a strong connection between simplicity (which most of us know very little about) and God's kingdom (something else that most of us know very little about). So let's start by breaking down this charge of Jesus to seek first God's kingdom, and then work to gain a better understanding of what God's kingdom really is.

Seek first. Jesus calls us to seek first God's kingdom (see Matthew 6:33). Seek first. This is a call to action and priority. In two simple words Jesus let us know that there is work for us to do and that it is important work—the most important work. Jesus does not mince words, nor does he want us to be confused on the matter. If we're going to get the rest of life right, meaning that we approach it, experience it, and live into it in the ways that God hopes for us, then we need to do *this* first. Seek first.

God's kingdom. God's kingdom is a topic of much theological debate, but for the sake of this study on simplicity, we will define it in terms of God's present and active work in the world, especially as it reflects and relates to heaven. We are invited to help bring about God's kingdom here on earth, as it is in heaven. We are called to work with God to make known his desires and priorities as we live out our earthly lives as sons and daughters of the King. So when we *seek first God's kingdom*, we're committing ourselves to living a life of prioritizing God, God's ways, God's wants for the world, and sharing God's heart for the world with the world.

And. The word *and* serves as a conjunction, connecting two thoughts or ideas. You know this—you're a college student after all. In this instance we are to understand that *seeking first God's kingdom* is not the end of the matter. There's more to this story. As we *seek first God's kingdom* there is something else that will happen. *And* serves as an equal sign in an equation that has *seek first God's kingdom* on one side and *all these things will be added unto you* on the other side. And.

All these things. In the context of this passage found in Matthew 6, a section on not worrying, found within the larger context of Jesus' first public address known as the

Sermon on the Mount, Jesus is talking about the muchness and manyness of his day.

> Therefore I tell you, do not worry about your life, what you will eat or drink; or about your body, what you will wear. Is not life more than food, and the body more than clothes? Look at the birds of the air; they do not sow or reap or store away in barns, and yet your heavenly Father feeds them. Are you not much more valuable than they? Can any one of you by worrying add a single hour to your life?
>
> And why do you worry about clothes? See how the flowers of the field grow. They do not labor or spin. Yet I tell you that not even Solomon in all his splendor was dressed like one of these. If that is how God clothes the grass of the field, which is here today and tomorrow is thrown into the fire, will he not much more clothe you—you of little faith? So do not worry, saying, "What shall we eat?" or "What shall we drink?" or "What shall we wear?" For the pagans run after all these things, and your heavenly Father knows that you need them. (Matt. 6:25–32)

Now, to be sure, the concerns Jesus is addressing in this passage are far more basic and central to what we need for life than what was addressed in the previous chapter on muchness and manyness And yet he also knew that if he didn't address these most basic of needs, the people wouldn't be able to focus on what he was saying or what he was attempting to prioritize for them—God's kingdom.

Now, Jesus didn't dismiss these concerns, but instead attempted to help the people understand that God is well aware of the needs of his children, so if they (and we) can focus on him and his kingdom, then *all these things* will be tended to as well.

Will be added. I think this phrase is misleading because in our consumeristic society we understand this to mean that if we focus on God and his priorities then he will give us what we want. I think this phrase could be better understood as *will be prioritized*, or even *will be taken care of in God's way*. In order to clarify that what happens on this side of the equation: *seek first God's kingdom and . . .* is not a *this-for-that* kind of transaction as we understand them. Instead, as we turn our attention and affection to the things of God, he will give us what we need—and not necessarily what we want. Remember, he's the God of the universe, not some cosmic Santa Claus. He knows us better than we know ourselves, and knows far better than we do what we need.

Unto you. What results from the *seek first God's kingdom and all these things shall be added* equation has both personal and communal ramifications. Our personal, and communal, willingness to *seek first God's kingdom* will not only impact us as individuals, but as a society as well. So the good that comes from our simplistic and united focus upon the things of God will bring about God's results in our lives, as well as the world in which we live.

It's not hard to see the kind of multiplying force that could be unleashed if we were willing to commit to this one thing.

Learn to Do Nothing

In many ways, the invitation to live simply by seeking first the kingdom of God is an invitation to do nothing. You might be thinking, *But wait, that's not what you just said. You didn't say to do nothing; you said to seek first God's kingdom.* And you're right. But in our noisy, busy, crowded world, where we are often defined by what we have, what we do, and who's on our team, the only way we're going to be able to really implement this new way of thinking and living is by learning to do nothing.

Like so many of the things we have talked about in this book, learning how to *do nothing* is something that most of us will have a hard time doing. We're *Americans* after all. We've been raised to be doers. We recognize that we live in a culture that defines us more by what we do, rather than who we are. Simple social economics would suggest that to *do nothing* would equate to being nothing. And nobody wants to be viewed as a nothing.

But this is the way of social economics in the world, not God's kingdom. If we're going to be about God's kingdom, as God's children and committed followers of Jesus, then we're going to need to simplify our lives, and this will require that we learn how to do nothing. By doing nothing, we are awakened to the social economics of our day and how they come into direct opposition with God's. We are also challenged to see that no matter how good our work, how great our relationships, or how well-intentioned our motives, if we're not *seeking first God's kingdom* then we are focused on the wrong things. It may very well be that God brings all of the aforementioned back into your world in similar ways and weights of importance. And he may not.

The key is that we're looking to God to set our priorities, while also giving us his understanding and perspective on each matter, which ultimately changes everything.

Learn to Keep Silent

Yep. I know what you're thinking: *First you tell us to be about God's kingdom and sharing the good news with others, but then you tell us not to do anything, and now you tell us to be silent. What gives!?* In similar fashion to learning what we learn in *doing nothing*, we must also practice creating space for God as we learn to *say nothing*. Simplicity not only frees us from feeling the need to *do* something in order to be of any good to anyone, but also from the need to *say* anything to be of any use to God and his purposes. Yes, it may seem counterintuitive to *be quiet about God*, but it's only when our words become simple that we learn how and when to use our words to the glory of God.

In silence, we are better able to hear the voice of God and better discern his leading in our lives. In silence we are freed to hear his plans and agenda, for our lives and the world, over and above our own. In our distracted existence we consistently fail to recognize the ways God is trying to communicate with us. The still, small voice of God is drowned out by the complexity of our lives and the noise, hurry, and crowds that we surround ourselves with. In learning to keep silent, we communicate to God that we want to hear from him. We want what he wants—or at least, we want to want it.

In the silence, we are also better able to hear from others, and discern when and how God might like us to speak into their lives—and when he would prefer us to stay quiet. In our *doer* culture we have come to believe that our words are just as important as our actions. In fact, in some settings and situations, it is words that we believe can be of the best assistance. We want to help our friends, we want to stand up for the rights of others, and we think that our words are the vehicle that God can use to help bring about change. But we too often forgo actually consulting God about any of this. We jump right to using our words—relying on our own wisdom, insight, and strength—rather than God's. As we learn to be silent, we choose a more simple way of living and being, and wait on the leading of God before we are moved into action or words of any kind.

Inward Reality with an
Outward Expression

Let's be clear. The practice of simplicity is far more than reigning in our actions and words. Simplicity, in many ways, is slowing down and silencing our outer world so that we might create space to work on our inner world, which will ultimately bring a reshaping to our outer world as well. Foster wrote, "The Christian Discipline of simplicity is an inward reality that results in an outward lifestyle. Both the inward and the outward aspects of simplicity are essential."[4] But it's often easier, and even essential, to quiet and simplify what we can on the exterior so that work can begin on the interior.

When we create space for God to simplify our existence, we are inviting him to bring order to the chaos. We are offering our lives to God and giving him permission to reorder and rearrange everything—on the inside and out. When this happens, we make ourselves better available to be agents of God in the here and the now. We don't have to worry about what our actions look like or our words sound like. Nor do we need to be concerned with the ultimate outcome. When we avail ourselves to God through the practice of simplicity, we are freed up to be faithful and obedient to his leading in our life—and we trust that he is both aware of and ultimately for whatever and wherever that leads. According to Foster, "If what we have we receive as a gift, and if what we have is to be cared for by God, and if what we have is available to others, then we will possess freedom from anxiety. This is the inward reality of simplicity."[5] It all leads to an inner peace and joy that we cannot manufacture. Only God can produce this within us.

Foster expounded on this when he wrote, "Experiencing the inward reality liberates us outwardly. Speech becomes truthful and honest. The lust for status and position is gone because we no longer need status and position. We cease from showy extravagance not on the grounds of being unable to afford it, but on the grounds of principle. Our goods become available to others."[6] Simplicity leads to freedom—freedom from all of the complexities of this world and of our own making. A more simple existence is a more honest expression of our true self, which puts us in position to be more usable in the hands of God, and helps us to become a more peaceful, single-minded, wholly devoted follower of Jesus.

Simplicity Cannot Become an Idol

A word of caution, however, before we move on: the spiritual disciplines, just like anything else, have the potential to become an idol in our lives. Yes, even the spiritual disciplines.

As was mentioned earlier in this book, although the spiritual disciplines are the work that we do in order to position ourselves in a more humble and moldable posture before God, we are never guaranteed any kind of result. Our role in the process is to choose God and engage in practices that will help us to be more in line with what he wants, but that is where our work ends.

If our formation, standing, and relationship with God were solely dependent upon our effort, then God would be in a position where he was subject to us. We could conceivably manipulate him with our good deeds and good words to produce whatever we desired. In many ways, that relational paradigm would play right into the hands of our Adversary—and the noise, hurry, crowds, muchness and manyness that we've been talking about throughout the course of this book.

In many respects, we can look to the counsel of James, the brother of Jesus, and see what he had to say about a similar (yet different) faith and deeds tension:

> What good is it, my brothers and sisters, if someone claims to have faith but has no deeds? Can such faith save them? Suppose a brother or a sister is without clothes and daily food. If one of you says to them, "Go in peace; keep warm and well fed," but does nothing about their physical needs, what good is it? In the same way, faith by itself, if it is not accompanied by action, is dead.
>
> But someone will say, "You have faith; I have deeds."
>
> Show me your faith without deeds, and I will show you my faith by my deeds. You believe that there is one God. Good! Even the demons believe that—and shudder.
>
> You foolish person, do you want evidence that faith without deeds is useless? Was not our father Abraham considered righteous for what he did when he offered his son Isaac on the altar? You see that his faith and his actions were working together, and his faith was made complete by what he did. And the scripture was fulfilled that says, "Abraham believed God, and it was credited to him as righteousness," and he was called God's friend. You see that a person is considered righteous by what they do and not by faith alone.
>
> In the same way, was not even Rahab the prostitute considered righteous for what she did when she gave lodging to the spies and sent them off in a different direction? As the body without the spirit is dead, so faith without deeds is dead. (James 2:14–25)

Faith and deeds, or faith and action, work together to accomplish what God desires. We do the work that God asks or requires of us, and then we put faith and trust in him to do whatever it is he desires. The results are up to him. The finished product is not ours to determine.

Let us now consider what it might look like to begin to incorporate the discipline of simplicity into our daily lives.

CHAPTER TWELVE

Learning to Be Content in a Culture of Abundance

Keep your lives free from the love of money and be
content with what you have, because God has said,
"Never will I leave you; never will I forsake you."
—Hebrews 13:5

[Jesus] calls all who would follow him to a joyful
life of carefree unconcern for possessions.
—Richard Foster, *Celebration of Discipline*

Like Jesus, we must learn to say that God is enough.
—Gary Holloway, *You Might Be Too Busy If . . .*

The first encounters that I recall with simplicity happened
toward the end of my college career and first couple
of years after graduation. They were not experiences that I

chose for their simplistic nature, but for other reasons altogether. The summers after my junior and senior years of
college I worked as a camp counselor at a Christian camp in
rural northern Minnesota. The summer after my first year of
working as a campus ministry graduate assistant afforded me
the opportunity to spend a week training in Juarez, Mexico,
for my summer of ministry on an Indian reservation in Fort
Apache, Arizona. All of these experiences required that I be
light, mobile, and without anything that could easily get lost,
damaged, or stolen. A more simplistic way of life wasn't an
option as much as a necessity for these different experiences.

I'm sure this kind of experience is different for everyone,
but I was surprised at the different phases I experienced as
I was forced into a life apart from my belongings, my social
scenes, and my most significant relationships. In a lot of ways
it felt like I was going through withdrawal of some kind. At
first the silence and simplicity of my situation felt new and
freeing. But by the first few nights, the noises and lack of
distractions that I was used to filling the silence with became
evident and I felt alone, bored, and even a little rattled. After
the first few days to a week of struggling to adjust, it eventually happened. But periodically throughout these different
summer experiences there would be something that would
draw my attention back to the fact that I had become
detached from the things I had once clung to for security,
comfort, self-worth, and even my identity. In those moments
I felt free, but naked and afraid at the same time. It was clear
to me that there was a tension, even a battle, still happening
within me.

Richard Foster wrote:

> Contemporary culture lacks both the inward reality and
> the outward lifestyle of simplicity. We must live in the
> modern world, and we are affected by its fractured and

fragmented state. We are trapped in a maze of competing attachments. One moment we make decisions on the basis of sound reason and the next moment out of fear of what others will think of us. We have no unity or focus around which our lives are oriented.[1]

In my summer experiences—these early encounters with simplicity—my inward and outward realities were experiencing things that they'd never before experienced. This simplistic outward reality was causing my inward reality, which had been conditioned for more than twenty years to want the muchness and manyness of life, to go into identity-crisis mode. I liked having very little to care about, aside from the work that God was putting right in front of me each day, but I struggled regularly with the belief that I was missing out on something back in civilization.

I think these encounters with simplicity are not unique to me. I think these kinds of tensions are similar to the kinds of tensions you will feel as you begin to engage in the practice of simplicity. The difference for you is that you're not likely to be plunged into a situation that will require you to drop everything that currently consumes your life (although that could prove helpful), which will allow you the ability to take small, measured steps into the practice of simplicity. Let's look at some ways you might begin to engage this discipline.

Lean into God

The One True God should always inform our practice of simplicity. Gary Holloway wrote, "Direction for simplifying our lives comes out of that daily solitude and silence. In prayer, meditation, and resting with God we find that we must (and can) let go of things that burden us. Some of those things are literally things that we can do better without. The rest is inward stuff that we must let go."[2] If you want to know where to begin with this discipline, a great place to start is to ask God to reveal to you—through some of the disciplines you're already engaging—what has too much control in your life. God knows you, and knows what you can handle, and will likely illuminate something in your life if you allow him the space to speak.

One of the temptations will be for you to give up things that seem significant, but in actuality, don't have much control over you. You'll be persuaded to believe that because you're denying yourself these things (that don't really mean much to you) that you're doing the good work of simplicity. And because you're doing what you believe to be work, you'll wonder why it doesn't seem like God is doing anything on his end.

Remember, we have an Adversary who is cunning and deceptive. He is the one who has tricked us into believing that we need muchness and manyness in order to be happy. He is the one that doesn't want to see us find God, and experience any kind of success, through our practice of simplicity. Our first and best beginning is simply seeking the guidance and direction of Jesus.

Take It One Day at a Time

Another great idea is to take your early engagements with simplicity one day at a time. As you wake in the morning, or before you go to bed the night before, ask God to reveal to you at least one way you might honor him, and potentially experience him, by living more simply.

Rather than feel the weight and pressure that might come with believing that you need to give up something for the rest of your life (although there will likely come a time when God will lead you to practice simplicity at this level), see it as an experiment in which you are trying to see how much control this one thing has in your life—and how much you are challenged to lean into God in order to keep your focus on him on that particular day. As the day ends, spend some time thinking and praying about what God revealed to you throughout your day.

Trust God with What You Need

Trust is a hard thing for most of us to come by. Most of us have been exposed to some harsh realities in life and have seen enough ugliness in humanity to make us distrusting of most people. And if we've ever had an experience where we felt like God had let us down, then trusting him is going to be just as challenging. Even with some of our most basic of needs.

But this provides a great entryway for us into the practice of simplicity. Start each day with a simple prayer, asking God to take care of your needs for the day ahead. Ask him to help you to be able to distinguish between needs and wants, and see what you find. Take some time at the end of each day to reflect on how God has met your needs and explore the ways he surprised you.

Be Willing to Share What You Have

Learning to share what you have is a great way to practice simplicity. When you share what you have, you loosen the grip that you hold things with, which ultimately loosens the grip that those things have on you. Instead of seeing yourself as defender and protector of what you have (whether it is physical or something more intangible like your reputation), you learn to see yourself as a steward. Stewards still care about what happens to their things, and do their very best to take good care of them, but they ultimately recognize that they are not the owners of these items—God is.

What do you have that others can benefit from? What have you been holding on to that others might appreciate the chance to utilize or enjoy? How can you make more of what you have available to others?

Give Some Things Away

Another great way to practice the discipline of simplicity is to give some things away. A great place to start would likely be your closet. Not only is a closet a place for keeping the overabundance of clothing that most of us live with, but it often becomes the mini-storage space where we shove the items that we no longer want in our daily living space. We don't believe the items have lost their use to us, but we have enough other stuff keeping us preoccupied that we simply need to relocate some of the excess.

Take some time to look through your closet. Are there items that jump out at you as something you can give away? Do it! If you look at something and wonder what it is, or where it came from—add it to your give-away pile. Comb through your piles of jeans, your stacks of T-shirts, your button-ups, sweaters, and dresses, and identify any articles you've not worn in the last twelve months. Add them to the pile.

What does your closet look like now? Look at the pile you've created. Would you really miss any of the things in the pile if you were to get rid of it all? Before you pull anything out of the pile to stick back in your closet, prayerfully consider why you would do that.

And let us be clear, all of the vacant space you now find in your closet should *not* serve as a reason to go out and buy more items to fill it back up. Our exercise in simplicity cannot become the pathway by which we end up deeper entrenched in the pursuit of muchness and manyness.

Buy Only What Is Necessary

Necessary is a funny word in our affluent, North American culture. We are regularly convinced of the fact that we must have this or that. We assure ourselves that an upgrade is not only okay, but in fact the responsible thing to do.

Foster's words are enlightening and give us cause to pause before we make any future purchases. He wrote, "Simplicity is the only thing that sufficiently reorients our lives so that possessions can be genuinely enjoyed without destroying us."[3] He wrote of a necessary reorientation to our possessions, one that would help us to see them for what they really are—items not containing any magical or mystical powers that will bring lasting joy or good standing with others, but items to be enjoyed and shared. When we are able to get to this kind of understanding with regards to what we have, it will impact what we buy and why we buy it. When we are freed from the belief that our active participation in the greater consumer culture is what will bring us happiness, fulfillment, and a greater sense of self, we will find ourselves buying less and less.

Deal with Your Debt

Debt is one of the major ways our Adversary works in our contemporary, instant-gratification, consumeristic culture. He convinces us that we shouldn't have to wait to get what we want—what we *need*. With the promise of meeting or even exceeding our expectations regarding the levels of joy and contentment our new purchase will provide, this Adversary tricks us into spending money that we don't have for fleeting feelings that quickly dissipate once our purchase is made. Feeling let down, and in need of another fix, we are tempted to buy more, bigger, and more expensive items without realizing that we are becoming ensnared in the never-ending consumeristic cycle.

Another great way of beginning to practice the discipline of simplicity is to assess and begin to deal with any debt that you might have. For many college students, school debt is going to be a part of your reality. But I think too many college students simply accept that they're going to have to take out loans for their education and therefore opt to let the debt pile on without much awareness or concern for what it means for their future. Decide to get educated on your school debt and prayerfully consider if there might be some creative ways that you can work to minimize (instead of unknowingly maximize) your debt.

What other debt do you have? A car payment? Credit cards? If so, how can you make paying these debts down a priority? Every little bit helps. Identify unnecessary spending in your daily routine that you can eliminate and redirect the funds you save toward reducing your debt. Instead of buying coffee on the way to wherever you're going, make it at home. Pack your lunch and take it with you rather than choosing to eat out every day. If you're really feeling motivated, you might consider opting for a mass transit means of transportation instead of having your own car on campus (which can save you money on car payments, gas, insurance, and routine maintenance).

Debt is a great indicator that you are not living simply, but in fact, beyond your means. If you cannot afford something, the answer is not to buy it on credit, but to wait until you have the money to purchase it. In the meantime, as you're saving up to buy whatever it is that you think you need, create a little time and space for God to speak to you with regard to whether you really need that particular item or not. By limiting your spending to what you really need, you will, in turn, help reduce your debt load which ultimately frees you to go as God leads.

One of the biggest hindrances to following the will of God for our life is debt. It's like an anchor that keeps us tethered to a job (or jobs) that are strictly a means of income and assures that we're able to make each loan payment as they come due. I know too many college grads that are unable to follow their dreams and do what they feel God calling them to do because of the debt they have. When you reduce, or even eliminate, your debt, you free yourself to more easily follow the leading of God.

Avoid Unnecessary Words or Chatter

Much of what we've talked about in this chapter has had to do with honoring God through reconsidering and reducing your personal material world. But as we explored in the previous chapter, it's not just your material world that needs simplifying. God wants control of your entire life. God wants you to trust him with everything that makes up your life. This includes things like your reputation, your social status, and the way people think of you.

One of the easiest ways to practice simplicity in this area of your life is by learning to limit your words. Yes, this is a practice that has been mentioned before, in the disciplines of silence and solitude. This just goes to further illustrate how powerful and powerfully distracting your words can be. When you willingly choose to limit your words, and reduce the meaningless chatter that we all so readily participate in, you eliminate a lot of trouble and create a lot more space for God to speak into your existence. Put your trust in God to represent you in your silence and submission.

What are some ways you can simplify your life by speaking less? What are the contexts in which you most need to learn to control your tongue? Who are the people that you need to spend more time listening to and less time talking at? How can you find your identity in Christ alone and not the words you weave for the sake of trying to win favor, or save face, in the eyes of other people?

There are several other ways that the discipline of simplicity can be engaged, and my guess is that you've already begun to identify some possibilities for your life. Simplicity, just like any other discipline, is not about the discipline itself, but instead, what the practice has the potential to produce in your life. The With-God life is always the ultimate goal. Walking more closely with Jesus, and better being able to hear and discern his voice and leading, is what we hope our engagement of the disciplines will yield in us.

Conclusion

The classical Disciplines of the spiritual life call
us to move beyond surface-level living into the
depths. They invite us to explore the inner caverns
of the spiritual realm. They urge us to be the
answer to a hollow world.
—Richard Foster, *Celebration of Discipline*

God intends the Disciplines of the spiritual life
to be for ordinary human beings: people who
have jobs, who care for children, who wash dishes
and mow lawns. In fact, the Disciplines are best
exercised in the midst of our relationships with
our husband or wife, our brothers and sisters,
our friends and neighbors.
—Richard Foster, *Celebration of Discipline*

I f you've made it this far, I imagine you might now find
yourself in one of two places. One, you're excited to begin
to engage these spiritual disciplines in ways you hope will
yield new intimacy and spiritual fruit in your relationship
with Christ; or two, you're feeling overwhelmed by the fact
that the kind of With-God life you've long desired, although

seemingly more possible and less allusive than it once appeared, will come at a cost.

The truth of the matter is that once you've been educated to the fact that the With-God life requires more than just "read your Bible and pray" kinds of effort, you're likely to be both hopeful and dismayed. You're hopeful because you've long felt that the fruits of your efforts have been under-whelming; yet you believed there had to be more. And you're dismayed, both because you can't believe that those who have loved you and led you have only ever exposed you to this way of engaging your faith, and because you now realize that your relationship with God will require more (and not less) of you.

Yes, prayer and consistent Bible study are a part of the makeup of a healthy faith and growing spiritual life. But there are a lot of other disciplines through which God has created opportunity for us to engage and experience him. Disciplines to which most of us have never been exposed. Disciplines that seem to come into direct conflict with our cultural norms and priorities. Disciplines that our Adversary doesn't want us to know about, practice, or believe will yield anything in our life. But God has a way of using our consistent pursuit of him, through the regular practice of the spiritual disciplines, to grow something within us as he grows what's happening between us.

We Live in a World Full of Noise, Hurry, Crowds, and Confusion

If we want to experience God in new and profound ways, if we want him to do a work within us that is supernatural and beyond what we can personally manufacture, if we want God to use us in ways that will bring hope and change to a world in need, then we must be willing to pursue him in ways that we've previously not. We need to engage in more than half-hearted attempts at reading our Bible and praying. And it needs to start with addressing all of the distractions we face on a daily basis.

We live in a noisy world. A world that easily drowns out the still, small voice of God. Not because God is incapable of overcoming the noise, but because he chooses not to compete with it. He wants us to want him enough to be willing to take efforts that will turn down the noise we surround ourselves with, as well as the noise we contribute, such that we're better able to hear and recognize his still, small voice. If we might imagine a volume dial that represented the noise in our life, God is waiting for us to work at turning it down.

So he invites us into silence.

Similarly, if we could imagine a gas pedal that dealt with the pace of life that we often choose to live at, God would like to see us let up on the speed toward a slower, more intentional and sustainable level, so that we might better be able to sense his activity in our midst. Too many of us live life like we have the pedal to the metal—constantly racing from one thing to the next—and never really having the chance to be fully present or enjoy the different events of our life. The pace we set for ourselves, or that we allow others to dictate for us, often leaves little if any room for the things of God. And this includes how we might choose to fill much of our schedules with activities meant to grow and engage our faith, but because we are so consumed with doing, we are left with very little time and space to simply be—with God or with self.

So God offers us Sabbath rest.

And then there are the crowds. We are rarely alone. And if we're honest, that's the way many of us prefer it to be. We have likely never learned to be alone, or learned the value of being alone, so we've grown to do whatever it takes to avoid it. We work to fill our days with opportunities to be with others, and even when we're alone, tap into our technologies so that we can fill the silence and solitude with our digital crowds. Many of us struggle with the thought of being alone because we fail to believe that God will meet us in that quiet, lonely place, or instead we fear that indeed God might actually meet us there.

God waits for us in solitude.

Finally, there's the confusion that comes as a result of our obsession with muchness and manyness. We've been trained by a culture (that's been heavily influenced by our Adversary) to believe that we are what we own or what people think of us. We have learned to equate our reputation and/or possessions with our sense of self and self-worth. We've become so consumed with the pursuit of muchness and manyness that we leave little (if any) room for the things of God. We might say that we want to live the With-God life, or even make good efforts toward that end, but we allow ourselves to be overly consumed with the cares and priorities of our culture. If we want more of God, then we need to be willing to live counter to much of our North American culture. We need to bring under control our obsession with muchness and manyness. We need to find a better way.

God offers us the practice of simplicity.

We Create Space Because We Want to Experience the With-God Life

That's what this book has been about—finding a better way of life by creating more intentional space for God to speak and work and have his way. The With-God life doesn't just happen naturally. Even though we've been created by a relational God, as relational beings for a relationship with God and with others, we struggle to consistently prioritize our relationship with God or know how to effectively invest in that important relationship. We believe things should be different, but struggle to know how. We look for examples or models, but struggle to find them.

Then we learn that if we want to experience God, if we want to make much of God in our life such that we're changed and transformed—from the inside out—then we're going to have to reconsider everything about the ways we live and the priorities we keep. And, when we make this move, one of the first things we must recognize is that many of the ways of living in our contemporary world are not conducive to the With-God life. The noise, hurry, and crowds that define our culture, and bring shape to our lives, serve to consume every square inch of our being, leaving little to no room for God. Our obsession with muchness and manyness that we have adopted from our culture works against the With-God life, squelching the movement of God's Spirit and drowning out the activity of Jesus in our life.

So *this moment*—now—becomes our starting point. We must learn to deal with the chaotic world in which we live— both externally and internally. Because if we truly want more of God, we must make commitments that will help to create more space for him in our life. The ways we do this, the ways we create more space for God to speak and move within our lives, is by learning how to quiet the noise, slow the pace, regulate the crowds, and control the pursuit of muchness and manyness. We must choose to quit going with the flow and begin to swim upstream, fighting to cultivate a different kind of existence—both within us and around us, believing that it's the only way we're going to experience the With-God life in the ways that we desire.

We Do the Work That We Can and Leave the Rest to God

We have to make this choice for ourselves because the world will not choose it for us. We need to commit ourselves to certain kinds of practices that will help to facilitate the kind of space in our noisy, hurried, crowded, and chaotic world . that will prove to be fertile soil for the work of God. The spiritual disciplines are these practices. And the practices of silence, Sabbath, solitude, and simplicity are among some of the most important disciplines that we might engage with the specific intent of creating space for God.

But, we must be reminded that our consistent engagement of the spiritual disciplines does not guarantee us anything. The disciplines are not a magic formula that serves to get God to do what we want. Instead, the spiritual disciplines are a way of working with God on our own lives to better prepare our hearts and minds for the With-God life. The disciplines put us in a better space, a more workable posture, for God to do in us what he desires. These practices are our way of working with God to till the soil of our soul to more readily receive the seeds and tender work of God and God's Spirit within.

We do this work because we believe that God wants us to want him more than we want anything else in this world. He wants us to choose him. Day after day. Week after week. Year after year. He wants us to choose him and make him the number-one priority in our life. He will pursue us, but he won't compete for our attention or affection. That's not who God is and it's not how he works. He calls upon us to put forth effort that shows the true desires of our heart and the level of effort and countercultural measures we're willing to avail ourselves to in order to create space for him to move and have his way in our life.

But our work has its limits. There's only so much we can humanly do. We do the work that God gives for us to do and then trust that God will do the work that only he can do. And this is the challenge, and for many of us the struggle, with the spiritual disciplines. We've long been taught that if we work hard enough, if we learn more and practice, practice, practice, that we'll be able to accomplish anything we set our minds to. But that is not true in the case of the spiritual disciplines and the With-God life. We do our work, and trust that God will do his work, and are challenged to leave the results—the fruit, growth, and spiritual maturity—to the intended end that God desires for us in our lives.

And it is this very thing, this unique equation that involves us and God and not knowing and limited control, which all too often scares us away from consistently pursuing God through engaging the spiritual disciplines.

But, if we can stand in faith, and put our full trust in God as we choose to consistently pursue him through the practice of the different spiritual disciplines, then there's no telling where or when or how God will choose to work. But he will. He will work. He will do something new and amazing and altogether beyond us when we choose to make him the center of our lives day after day after day.

The With-God life is a journey toward the heartbeat of God. It's a journey that serves to bring shape, and make sense of, the rest of life. It's our one opportunity to experience God's coming kingdom here on earth and to be a part of his ongoing and unfolding work in our hurting world. It's an open invitation, to you and to me, to live with the One True God today—and every day.

Are you ready?

Notes

Introduction

1. Richard J. Foster, *Celebration of Discipline: The Path to Spiritual Growth*, revised ed. (San Francisco: Harper & Row, 1988), 7.

2. Dallas Willard, *The Divine Conspiracy: Rediscovering Our Hidden Life in God* (San Francisco: HarperSanFrancisco, 1998), 353.

3. Foster, *Celebration of Discipline*, 1.

4. Willard, *Divine Conspiracy*, 348.

Chapter One: Noise

1. Jun Young and David Kinnaman, *The Hyperlinked Life: Living with Wisdom in an Age of Information Overload* (Grand Rapids, MI: Zondervan, 2013), 15.

2. Dallas Willard, *The Spirit of the Disciplines: Understanding How God Changes Lives* (San Francisco: HarperSanFrancisco, 1988), 63.

3. Young and Kinnaman, *Hyperlinked Life*, 16.

4. Willard, *The Spirit of the Disciplines*, 163.

Chapter Two: Silence

1. Gary Holloway, *You Might Be Too Busy If . . . : Spiritual Practices for People in a Hurry* (Abilene, TX: ACU/Leafwood Publishers, 2009), 47.

2. Dallas Willard, *The Spirit of the Disciplines: Understanding How God Changes Lives* (San Francisco: HarperSanFrancisco, 1988), 164.

3. Rufus M. Jones, 1937—as found on page 54 of the Minutes of Iowa Yearly Meeting (Conservative), 132nd Annual Sessions. Seventh Month 28 to Eighth Month 2, 2009.

4. Frederick Buechner, *Telling Secrets: A Memoir* (San Francisco: HarperSanFrancisco, 1991), 117.

5. Willard, *The Spirit of the Disciplines*, 164.

6. Holloway, *You Might Be Too Busy If . . .* , 48.

7. Robert M. Mulholland, *Invitation to a Journey: A Road Map for Spiritual Formation* (Downers Grove, IL: InterVarsity, 1993), 137.

8. Holloway, *You Might Be Too Busy If . . .* , 48.

Chapter Three: Learning to Quiet Our Inner (and Outer) World

1. Thomas Merton, *Contemplative Prayer* (New York: Herder and Herder, 1969), 37.

Chapter Four: Hurry

1. Frederick Buechner, *Wishful Thinking: A Seeker's ABC* (San Francisco: HarperSanFrancisco, 1993), 95.

Chapter Five: Sabbath (Slowing)

1. Gary Holloway, *You Might Be Too Busy If . . . : Spiritual Practices for People in a Hurry* (Abilene, TX: ACU/Leafwood Publishers, 2009), 75.

2. Ibid., 88.

Chapter Six: Learning to Live with Greater Intention

1. Richard J. Foster, *Celebration of Discipline: The Path to Spiritual Growth* (San Francisco: Harper & Row, 1978), 1.

2. Ibid.

Chapter Seven: Crowds

1. Henri J. M. Nouwen, *The Way of the Heart: Desert Spirituality and Contemporary Ministry* (New York: Seabury Press, 1981), 9.

2. Ibid., 10.

Chapter Eight: Solitude

1. Gary Holloway, *You Might Be Too Busy If . . . : Spiritual Practices for People in a Hurry* (Abilene, TX: ACU/Leafwood Publishers, 2009), 31.

2. Richard J. Foster, *Celebration of Discipline: The Path to Spiritual Growth* (San Francisco: Harper & Row, 1978), 96.

3. Dallas Willard, *The Spirit of the Disciplines: Understanding How God Changes Lives* (San Francisco: HarperSanFrancisco, 1991), 160.

4. Henri J. M. Nouwen, *The Way of the Heart: Desert Spirituality and Contemporary Ministry* (New York: Seabury Press, 1981), 13.

5. Henri J. M. Nouwen, *Out of Solitude: Three Meditations on the Christian Life* (Notre Dame, IN: Ave Maria Press, 1974), 22.

6. Gary Thomas, *Sacred Pathways: Discover Your Soul's Path to God* (Grand Rapids, MI: Zondervan, 2010), 99.

7. Dietrich Bonhoeffer, *Life Together*, trans. John W. Doberstein (New York: Harper, 1954), 77.

Chapter Ten: "Muchness" and "Manyness"

1. Richard J. Foster, *Celebration of Discipline: The Path to Spiritual Growth* (San Francisco: Harper & Row, 1978), 80–81.

Chapter Eleven: Simplicity

1. Richard J. Foster, *Celebration of Discipline: The Path to Spiritual Growth* (San Francisco: Harper & Row, 1978), 86.

2. Ibid., 91.

3. Ibid., 87.

4. Ibid., 79.

5. Ibid., 88.

6. Ibid., 80.

Chapter Twelve: Learning to Be Content in a Culture of Abundance

1. Richard J. Foster, *Celebration of Discipline: The Path to Spiritual Growth* (San Francisco: Harper & Row, 1978), 80.

2. Gary Holloway, *You Might Be Too Busy If . . . : Spiritual Practices for People in a Hurry* (Abilene, TX: ACU/Leafwood Publishers, 2009), 53.

3. Foster, *Celebration of Discipline*, 84–85.